Deeds of Trust

Deeds of Trust

a true story

by Alesandra Rain

Deeds of Trust

Library of Congress Cataloging-in-Publication-Data

ISBN 0-9778040-0-3

Book Cover Design: Pete Peterson
www.popcreations.com

Aknowledgement

Deeds of Trust was a lifelong path - it just took ten years to write my memoir. It was in the midst of my horror, without a voice to express perceptions, that I took pen to paper. The evolution of my story has had many names and certainly grew in magnitude as the truth unfolded. But I had no idea what was happening or certainly what the outcome would be. It began as my way to heal – later it became a way for others to.

My journey was certainly full of many wrong choices. I did things I regret and chose people that should not have gained admittance to my world. But ultimately, each choice was mine and therefore I have had to live with the consequences.

What became clear was the tremendous value of the gift bestowed upon me. Not just in the nightmare itself, but also in the cherished individuals who helped me regain my footing. Ironically, it was the loss of faith that took me to my depths and the kindness of tender souls that brought me back.

Had it not been for the gentle hands that caught me time and again, I would have surely left this world. I have tremendous gratitude for a few unique individuals, for without their belief and sustaining energy I would not have persevered.

The kindness imparted by the staff of Cirque Lodge came at a time when I was desperate. They allowed me the extensive time necessary to regain my mind. Without their support and extreme generosity I would never have broken my addiction.

But it was through my rare connection with Andrea that *Label Me Sane* came into existence. She is my business partner and dear friend who is a remarkable woman that rose to a call. Andrea gave up a lucrative career and co-founded *Label Me Sane,* all because she knew in her heart it was the path she had to follow. She exuded belief in spirit and without her this mission would have fallen flat. It was her conviction and ultimate belief that made me continue through many disappointments and times of lost confidence.

And of course I have MJ – my sister and best friend who through it all gave me the belief and constant support to make the road back worth believing. Our friendship suffered devastating trials but it is stronger for it. God help anyone who tries to come between us again.

Smoke and Shadow

No, it is not the kind that swirls and sweeps
across the sky in search of meaning. Nor is it
a shadow that dances to the light of new moons.
The smoke is not that which detects location to save.
It is not of tobacco shared between friends.
The shadow passes by happy children at play
and disregards lovers in their richest hour.

This is the smoke, rather, that is conjured by man's
darkest region of mind. It is made of greed refuse and
fed with despair. It snuffs out all memory and marrow
of everything held dear. It is a shadow that shades
its target's lonely, waning eyes. Swallow the pill
and watch it grow over families
marriages
lives.

- M.J. Warrender

Deeds of Trust

Prologue

May 2005,
    *T*he interview was over and a sense of relief flooded through me. I knew the questions would be daunting and although Andrea had prepared me thoroughly, the adrenaline flowed freely. I had given dozens of interviews, but this reporter touched the heart of my story.

    I sat at my desk and my eyes floated through the room, seeing nothing but the ominous drawer, uncertain why I gave the documents a home. They were relegated to a box for seven years – why did I move them within reach? Behind a simple lock held the key to my past. The truth.

    Three years ago my life looked entirely different. Blackness permeated every aspect and cast its cloak over my soul. I wasn't sure I could make it back, or even if I wanted to. But some sliver of hope remained and pushed me through the darkness. What began as a journey to the very core of my being became the seedlings of an international corporation named *Label Me Sane*. We touch lives on a daily basis that are brought to hope through our connection. Each day I awaken with a renewed conviction to help others survive what I am convinced is the worst betrayal.

I swung my chair away from my desk and looked around my office. Transitory articles of our success serve as reminders of our purpose. When Andrea and I co-founded *Label Me Sane,* we never could have known how this amazing company would change the lives of so many. But what motivates all of us are the multitudes of telephone calls, letters and emails asking for help and thanking us for our efforts. They warm our hearts and fill the long hours that never seem to end.

How can so many people be suffering? I am driven to make sure each person receives a personal response. If the staff is too overloaded to answer every email, then I stay until everyone receives their lifeline. I can't take the thought that someone going through the nightmare does not receive a telephone call or email to keep them on this planet. I remember all too well how just the voice of someone who understood, kept me going through the worst of days.

I take as many calls as humanly possible, to both remind me of where I was only a few years ago, and also to extend the compassion and belief to another. It is human contact that takes us from the darkness back to the light. It is our conviction that each person can traverse their way through the hell to their elation in life's treasures that our clients feel. They know in their hearts that we can guide them back. They know we care.

Most of our staff has been on the drugs and therefore have the same passion as I do. They understand at their core how our clients are tormented. Many will work the weekends or late into the night, as Andrea and I do. I never have to ask, they just rise to their mission. I try to send them home when their eyes droop but they persist through their exhaustion. I hear time and again that *people are suffering, how can I leave?* We laugh, cry and do everything within our power to inspire those still caught in the agony. I feel so honored to be surrounded by such a loving group.

It is overwhelming, but just when I think my exhaustion is too deep to respond to yet another email or telephone request, someone will call, reaching for a lifeline and I am filled with passion to continue. Would they still be grateful if they knew the whole story?

My eyes hesitated momentarily on each piece of art that documented my travels and therefore a good portion of my adult life. The lifeline stopped nearly fourteen years ago.

I glanced around and remembered earlier times – my trip to Hong Kong, Hokkaido, Europe and the Grand Cayman Islands. I could feel a hint of the laughter and ease that symbolized how I moved through the world and approached life – all before I met him.

I looked out the window and saw the ocean shimmering. It looked so peaceful and comforting and reminded me of our wedding. I don't remember ever being that young or so inexperienced at the sinister aspects of life. I didn't know a black soul actually existed off the silver screen. I was a believer now.

The room began to squeeze me. I tried to shake off the foreboding sensations rippling through my skin, but knew it would be impossible if I stayed indoors. The sun and sand called.

I scribbled a note and left it on my desk. I was known for my midday walks. Andrea would understand - she knew me so well. I grabbed my sunglasses, pushed open the door and slipped down the back stairs. I kicked off my shoes and headed toward the blue.

The second my toes slid into the sand my heart lifted. I

pushed through the large dunes – craving the sensation of the waters edge. I pulled the salt air into my lungs and let my hair whip wildly in the strong breeze.

There were two small sailboats bobbing on the horizon, looking perfectly natural on the edge of the world. Throngs of seagulls filled the air, full of urgent calls. They were seeking food – I sought peace. I reached the soft waves in less than a minute and stood quietly. My thoughts were full of the past.

A few gulls stayed close, convinced I represented sustenance. Their dedication and tenacity brought a smile as I realized the memories couldn't hurt me anymore. I could go back without being consumed.

I picked up my pace, determined to experience the freedom of movement. The birds eventually realized that I promised nothing nourishing and abandoned me in search of a better provider.

I was left with my thoughts and the quietude of a perfect Southern California day as I pushed around a jagged rock cliff face and found my quiet spot up high - a safe pinnacle. From this distance I knew it was possible to reflect. The soft clouds floated above my head, taking me to a different time. I could imagine the sky on the day I met him, how innocent it all seemed. How could I ever have known how my life would be altered?

Chapter 1

$\mathcal{A}$ good con is woven like a tight web, much like a spider's trap. It seems safe initially, then closes in around you. Deceit can wrap its tentacles so tightly that the truth is obscured. By the time the degree of danger is recognized, it is much too late.

At least for me that is exactly how it developed – slowly and with great precision. It unfolded over an extended period of time with total dedication.

The adage "love is blind" isn't exactly accurate. It is more that love can create a justification for outpoints in character.

Should I have seen the tidal wave coming?
Probably.

But like most storms of magnitude, it closed in quickly and with power.

Chapter 2

I met the man of my dreams in 1991. Mark Young was
unlike any other – he knew me in a way that was uncanny. It
was as if we had known each other many lifetimes, creating a
comfort and ease from day one.

At 6'5" Mark walked with an air of confidence. He was
drafted as a pitcher for the Milwaukee Brewers right out of
high school, and seemed to view the world from the height of
a pitcher's mound - on slightly elevated ground. It wasn't arrogance but rather confidence that governed his demeanor. His
boyish charm, dark brown hair, and crystal blue eyes completed
a formidable package.

I stood 5'10" and appeared the ideal woman for Mark.
Although I had been injured young in life and had undergone
numerous reconstructive surgeries to my extremities, my body
healed well and I wore my beauty effortlessly. My thick, long
brown sugar colored hair and flawless complexion complimented my elegant features and long lean body.

My beauty developed later in life and as a result, I was
aware of how the world responded to appearance – but also

how truly deceptive it could be. Beauty does not make one whole. It could only be used as a tool to demonstrate what lie beneath.

Mark often complimented my willingness to accept people based on who they were, rather than what they seemed to offer. He loved my subtle movement, using my looks to open doors and yet my unwillingness to rest on laurels that could not be substantiated.

It wasn't his presence that won me over but rather his certainty. He laughed easily and filled rooms with the rich sound. Mark seemed content to have quiet dinners in hole-in-the-wall café's or spend a day hiking the cliffs in La Jolla, California, as long as we were together.

Like myself, Mark loved animals and on one of our first dates took me to the Wild Animal Park. The quiet world of nature filled him with awe, as it did me. Yet he understood the other side of me that craved the city and all its treasures.

In late December of 1991, we had been dating about eight months and I had a long business trip in New York City. It was an exhausting agenda of complicated negotiations and by weeks end, Mark could hear my fatigue deepening. He surprised me and flew to New York and demanded I take a few days off to both enjoy the city and rest. Mark did this often - taking control. It lured me in and made me feel feminine. This was a new experience for me.

We discovered the electric city blanketed in snow, and allowed the power of the live stage to re-energize me. It was idyllic.

His gifts were always the perfect blend of simple elegance, as I preferred timeless treasures rather than trendy baubles. We moved through the world, whether casual or formal, with a synergistic energy that convinced me we could

7

traverse any segment of life together.

Conflict was non-existent and that should have made me wary, but instead it only reinforced my belief that my method of choosing previous partners was flawed.

Mark honored my need for friends and family and was particularly supportive of my relationship with my twin sister MJ. She is an eternal hippy educated from an Ivy League School who is also a musician and a poet. He was careful to not overstep or crowd, or I would have surely limited our time together. Instead, he gave me all the room I needed and yet withdrew ever so slightly, making me reach for him.

Chapter 3

*T*he first year held a near perfect harmony. Mark took me to Hawaii and spared no expense to ensure we sailed, snorkeled and enjoyed every moment. The evenings were full of rich conversation drifting between various issues with confidence.

He was always interested in MJ's life and laughed at the hours we spent talking on the phone. He knew my sister was an integral part of my personality. Twins have a unique spiritual connection that can't be defined.

When Mark met MJ for the first time, he was kind and tender and stayed only long enough to be polite, then escaped so we could have our time together.

MJ seemed to have reservations about Mark. She never verbalized them and I never engaged her. The words that were never spoken should have said it all. Instead I let the undercurrent remain and followed my heart.

But it wasn't until 1992 when he asked me to go into business that my world shifted – but I didn't feel the rocking. Instead, I felt lulled. That day will hold forever in my mind – he orchestrated it perfectly and like a skilled musician, he played me.

•   •   •

I was extremely secure in my intelligence – I had a certainty in business and an ability to initiate and nurture corporations into successful ventures. I devoted a decade to launching a branch of our family company and longed to leave industrial sales and the world of engineering. Years working around hazardous chemicals left me yearning to work in an environment that was aesthetic. My career path was undetermined, but continuing my college education was paramount.

The ambiguity of my future combined with a deep love for Mark, left me exposed. As a predator stalks prey, he waited patiently for just the right moment to pounce.

Chapter 4

Mark was a real estate developer and had a small company that renovated single-family homes in San Diego. Although he had twenty years experience and vast success in real estate, he had not been able to fully materialize his dream of expanding the San Diego renovation market into a sizeable enterprise. Mark could take a dilapidated home that was unfit for occupancy and transform it into a sweet haven. Each home held its period in time, but would be renovated into a gem with all the modern conveniences. Of course he was rewarded handsomely for his efforts as many properties could be purchased for pennies on the dollar and then sold at the top of the market due to the upgrades.

The time to renovate a home could easily take up to six months, and that was only if the property was not in the Coastal Commission zone in a beach community. Then of course the added permits and engineering could easily add another year to the project.

Mark stayed in the first time buyer range and purchased small Victorian jewels inland that could be fixed and turned quickly. The property would remain in his ownership about nine months on average and took an inordinate amount of cash that limited his growth.

He was aware of my significant financial holdings and therefore of my intention to take several years off before choosing my next career path.

He began asking my help on subtle things such as landscaping and interior décor. Each suggestion would be implemented before we retoured his properties. He would compliment my choices and reach again. My ego was duly responsive and with each request the hook settled deeper. Eventually it proceeded to architectural layouts and coastal commission plans for upcoming projects. Before long his objective was superimposed over my own dreams.

When he asked me to become his business partner it was wrapped in a wedding proposal. I remember the day well. I should – it altered the course of my life.

Chapter 5

It was an exquisite summer day. The sky was an endless palette of blue and the gentle winds constant. We were spending the day in Balboa Park, acres of land and architecture built in 1915 for the world expo in San Diego. It was on the bridge between the park and the city that Mark asked me to marry him. I stopped and couldn't breathe. My two previous marriages flashed through my mind and a look of doubt crossed my face. He put his arms around me.

He said simply, "I'll continue asking and you answer only when you're ready."

My heart skipped and I was still floating above the city when he began talking again.

"You're a natural in renovations you know?" He said it softly, without any expectation.

"Thank you." I was still a bit out of body from the marriage proposal and gladly moved on to safe territory.

"I know you want to go back and finish your Bachelor's and then go to graduate school, but what about after?" He asked earnestly.

"I was planning on taking a couple of years off while

I'm studying, as I haven't decided between psychology and international business. I think the choice will come to me as I finish. I just feel the need to complete my studies. I never could after the accident and I just need to." I wanted his approval.

Mark knew that when I was 19, I was involved in a serious auto accident due to a drunk driver. I was studying under a scholarship and had to quit college to spend years undergoing reconstructive surgeries on my legs. My education was abruptly discontinued and after regaining my health, I went into the family business. Not finishing my studies was a life regret and the thought continually rose up that I had to finish.

"That's terrific! You should. You have an amazing mind. I was just thinking…" He hesitated.

"Thinking what?" I prompted.

"What would you feel about partnering up on some renovations?" He let the question hang.

"I'm not sure what you mean." My stomach felt tight.

"Well, I was just considering that while you are discovering your new career, we could work together and renovate a few homes. I'm great at raising money and locating properties. Clearly you have an eye for design and you don't have a problem with architectural drawings or engineering." He kept walking but I could feel his nervousness.

"I don't know Mark. My parents built a company together and it monopolized the family. I really want a relationship separate from my career." I felt like I let him down.

"You wouldn't be working with me. I'll stay off the construction sites. Whatever you decide I'll honor, promise." He crossed his heart like a boy scout.

It was the next portion that hooked me.

"I really see tremendous potential to create a special company if we teamed up. I'm incredible at raising money and working with investors. But you are a gifted business-woman, you started a new division of the family business and made it international with multi-millions in sales in just a few years. My skill set is truly working with investors. I can put deals together but need someone I can trust. You could run the expansion of the company while I work on the funding. Please consider it. You can help me for one year and wait on returning for your studies. Then you can go to any University you like without the concern of future income. It really could work."

I don't know when I agreed but before the walk was over, we were business partners. I had a marriage proposal from the man I loved, and a new career opportunity. My education had waited this long. It could wait for one more year. I went home feeling that my life couldn't be any richer.

•   •   •

It only took me a few months before I agreed to marry Mark. We had been dating about 1 - 1/2 years and fell into an easy rhythm, seeing each other whenever possible. It was difficult at times due to my busy schedule, as I was preparing to close my company, leaving my travel itinerary congested.

He never pushed me to alter my calendar but somehow found a way to mingle with mine, in perfect unison. He began offering to stay with my two cats, Selsie and Zeff, when I was out of town. Each time I returned home they were fully satiated, clearly receiving tender care from Mark.

My cats had been with me for over ten years and were very much my furry children. Mark found it humorous but honored the connection and babied them as his own. It made me love him more.

•   •   •

When he began asking to borrow money to complete housing projects for our future, I happily acquiesced. Although we hadn't formally formed the new corporation, it was agreed that any existing properties would be transferred into the new business as soon as I closed my company. I trusted him and we were to be married soon. I had fallen deeply in love with this man and just rode the wave.

Chapter 6

Shortly after I accepted his marriage proposal, I was planning the wedding. It all happened very naturally and with tremendous skill. I never felt so loved or understood by another living soul.

He didn't dwell on my words - it was nothing quite so obvious. Mark expressed interest in my dreams, fears and future. He didn't hesitate to disagree with my views but always contradicted me with respect. Opposing views were given in a way that made me consider his perspective, even if I rarely changed mine. It felt like the uniting of brilliant minds, with the opportunity to truly express myself in a way I had not with another man.

In the past, my intelligence had caused an underlying conflict. I'm quite sure it was because I never chose anyone who was my intellectual equal. Instead, my choices had been riddled with rather conventional men, as I had a mistaken belief that I needed someone less complex to counter my complicated layers. It took the experience with Mark to make me realize how truly distorted my choices had been, including my marriage to him.

A close friend helped me plan every detail of the wedding. The most tedious part was finding my dress, for I knew it had to be unconventional, elegant and completely unique. Yet each shop we visited only had the traditional wedding gowns. One afternoon I was watching three women up on the viewing platform, each in different versions of the traditional attire. They looked so happy with their choices and their mothers purred in agreement.

I wanted to laugh, as it was impossible to imagine myself in a puffy white dress with a long train and veil. I would feel like an imposter. I just wasn't orthodox. Maybe it was the fact that it was my third marriage, but somehow my spirit felt it had to have a unique expression.

When we found the dress, my spirit soared. It was the deepest shade of black velvet, off the shoulders with a narrow body, and long white gloves. It had simple, elegant lines while still clearly untraditional, as it was black.

How could I ever have known the color of my dress would foretell the future of my marriage?

·　　　·　　　·

Before the wedding, Mark suggested he move into my home as we were together nearly every night. My travel schedule was tight and it seemed the natural progression. After all, we would be married soon.

Chapter 7

*T*here are always clues to one's true nature. Some are subtle and others overt – it's a matter of paying attention and facing the inconsistencies. It doesn't matter how skilled the con, their inner reality surfaces at moments we never expect.

Mark certainly let me see snippets into his darkness. Some were flagrant gaps. I chose to ignore them, as I wanted to believe. This choice sent me on a downward spiral that nearly killed me.

My father always used to say -

In order to see the truth it is important to turn off the sound. Actions speak volumes - if we're listening.

The first episode occurred early in our relationship. In hindsight I feel foolish for not walking away, but at the time I gave him a chance to explain. That is another lesson I have learned to my core – some things cannot be explained away. They are authentic in themselves and should stand as such.

Chapter 8

Mark and I had been dating about six months before the first major outpoint surfaced. Our relationship was near perfection, with only minor moments of discomfort. I had spent the night at his home and woke him early the next morning to walk me to his underground parking garage. He kissed me goodbye and I slid into my car to leave. I rolled down the window and started my engine. Mark began walking back to the elevator.

Just as I started to pull out of the parking spot, I noticed a sizable woman struggling to get into her compact car. She was carrying a large purse and a briefcase with long straps that kept slipping off her shoulder. She strained to claim the papers spilling from her briefcase.

I was about to ask her if she needed some help but before the words rolled off my lips, I saw Mark look at her with contempt and mutter loudly,

"It's disgusting to see anyone who doesn't give a shit about their looks! Don't you care that you look like a fucking cow?"

Mark's cruelty slammed my mind into the concrete wall. I was so shocked that words failed me. The woman burst into tears and threw everything into her front seat. Her window was open and her sobs were clearly heard as she drove off.

I couldn't believe what I had just witnessed. I yelled to Mark but he didn't hear me as the elevator door closed and swallowed his frame. I was seething at his callous and cruel remark!

Could this conceivably be the same man who was so tender a few moments ago?

He walked away with an arrogant stride as if he was saying good morning to a neighbor.

I was in a state of shock. I drove home in a stupor, without any awareness of the road, appalled by Mark's attack. I could only imagine the anguish that woman felt. The contradictions in Mark's behavior were crashing wildly in my mind.

I steeled myself that whatever his excuse, I would not see him again. His behavior was too worrisome and indicative of a very disturbed man.

Chapter 9

I spent the rest of the day at my office, and tried to put Mark out of my mind. Later that evening I went home and stared at the phone for a few minutes trying to decide how best to end the relationship. I wasn't sure whether I wanted to talk to him again or not. I decided not and turned away. The phone rang. I hesitated but answered.

"Hi Alesandra, it's Mark."

I fell silent.

"Alesandra – you there?"

"Yeah, I'm here," My tone was clipped.

"Whoa, is something wrong?" He sounded like the gentle man, not the beast.

"You're kidding right?" I began to berate Mark over the incident in the garage.

After recounting what had happened, Mark spoke in a contrite voice,

"Wow, I never thought of it like that. Shit, it was cruel wasn't it? I wish I could find her to apologize, but I've never seen her in the building before. I completely understand why you are so angry with me."

"Huh?" Was all I could say.

"Damn, I have some things to work on, don't I? Please, give me the chance to become a better person." He spoke in a completely earnest tone.

My mind was whirling with confusion. Maybe I judged him too harshly. I was starting to feel guilty, and I was so sure of myself.

"Are you there?" Mark said softly.

"Yeah, I'm here." I was really confused.

"Do you want to see me again? I'd understand if you didn't."

"Okay." I responded.

•   •   •

Mark was careful not to make such an overt mistake again. I continued on with our relationship thinking I had a man who wanted to address his shortcomings. The truth was far more sinister.

Chapter 10

The next few months were a mad rush to close my company while establish the office for our new venture together.

Monica, my assistant, joined us from my previous business. She was extremely diligent, easy to work with and fiercely loyal. Monica had a natural design eye that would prove invaluable in renovating homes.

In late 1992, we incorporated Develacor, acquired office space, automated the company and began to hire a staff. It was horribly tedious but within a few months we were in full swing.

Our office suite held two entrances, one that allowed access for the construction crews and the main entry that showcased the elegant furnishings for any potential investor. An archway separated the divisions and held two girls, Tina and Lora, who handled reception and general office duties while assisting Mark.

The investment side held Mark, any personnel to process the loans and the conference room. On the other side of the archway held construction, design, accounting and my offices with Monica. This kept each division running separately, while allowing easy communication.

Develacor was the corporation the industry was familiar with. It paid all salaries, carried the majority of the debt and owned the bulk of the properties we purchased. We had another company that purchased the properties with severe structural damage, but Develacor was the main corporation.

Investors wrote their checks or wired their funds into our Trust account, and in turn the money was wired to the Title Company to close escrow. Any remaining monies were disbursed as dictated in the escrow instructions.

Money sat in the Trust Account for very short periods of time, as the moment we received money from an investor, the clock began to tick loudly on interest payments.

All the details regarding investors and funding fell to Mark. He had nearly twenty years experience working with investors and negotiating through the piles of documents that encompassed a real estate purchase.

His main responsibility was to raise any funds necessary for the life of the deal. This included the purchase price, closing costs and any sales commissions paid to locate the property, all costs associated with the renovation, the marketing time to sell the property once it was renovated and the interval in escrow once the property was sold. The perfect scenario was receiving the required funds from Mark's investors, and in turn closing escrow immediately. This timing was crucial and rarely worked perfectly.

Our corporation purchased all the properties and was issued a Grant Deed, as we were the legal owner. All the other money we required was broken down into three portions.

The first and largest portion of the money to be raised was for the purchase of the properties. Mark was able to buy them for pennies on the dollar as they were in horrendous condition. Whoever invested in this received a "1st Trust Deed." They were the most secured, meaning that if for some reason we defaulted on the loan, they would be able to recover their investment since the house could be sold for enough to cover their Trust Deed. The interest rates paid for this first segment was less than anyone who invested after them.

The requirements of the second portion, or the "2nd Trust Deed" had to be sufficient to pay all interest payments on the 1st Trust Deed and the 2nd Trust Deed during the duration of the deal. It also had to include a development fee to our company as well as a finder's fee to the agent who located the property.

The development fee was critical to maintain our company, as we had to cover all the salaries, office lease, utilities and any other affiliated costs until the property sold.

Usually the 2nd Trust Deed took a leap of faith on the part of the investor, as the property would not have sufficient equity to cover their Trust Deed until after it was renovated. In its initial state, the property wasn't worth much more than what was on the 1st Trust Deed. But once the property was renovated, the value of the home increased dramatically and the investor was more than secured. Second position investors interest rates were higher due to the risk.

The last investor would receive a "3rd Trust Deed." The money Mark raised for this was required for the renovation phase. It included all construction costs, architectural fees, city permits and any other ancillary expenses. The interest rate for this portion was the highest as this investor was taking the highest risk. They received a healthy interest rate but had to wait until the property sold to receive their money.

Some investors preferred the last position due to the

higher interest rates, but this is where Mark often ran short in the early months of our company. He needed me to invest the construction funds as the company was growing quickly and he couldn't find sufficient investors to carry the position that was most exposed.

But within the first six months I discovered that if the rates of return Mark gave were too high, then when the property sold there would be either nothing left for our company or the investor in last position. Because a Trust Deed secured most investors, if the property lost money, the house could not be sold unless the investor took a "Short Sale."

A Short Sale occurs when the funds netted from the sale of the property is insufficient to repay the Trust Deeds against the property. Therefore, the money would be paid out and a Trust Deed holder would come up short. If the investor refused to take less than the actual Trust Deed amount, thus a short sale, we would either have to find a way to come up with the loss to close escrow, or let the sale go and hope for a higher offer.

Rarely would a property sell for an amount above the original offer, which left the individual in last position only partially paid. So Mark's initial estimates would haunt us for the life of the deal. If he made any errors in his calculations, there would be no way to make up the loss. Therefore Mark took his time with estimates and provided Monica and I an assessment for performance which we in turn adhered to with the contractors.

Chapter 11

I did not have sufficient experience with raising money from investors or estimating construction costs. My expertise was in managing work crews and taking the project through the construction phase. That is where Monica and I excelled, working with city permits, architectural teams and hiring the crews necessary to complete the work. It was all the details on the other side of the office archway that monopolized our time.

The initial fund raising was tedious for Mark, but he thrived on this. *Making the Deal* was his thing. He loved it. It was a game to him. A game he was gifted at.

The life of the project fell to me. We would have homes in various stages of renovation scattered all over the city. It was my job to ensure each project was proceeding on schedule and receiving the correct selections of paint, appliances, lighting and any other detail we had chosen. It was an exhausting process of initiating new projects while following the construction phases on each.

Once the property was completed, we hired the agents

to begin the marketing to put the home on the market. Then when the property was sold, Monica had to hire a crew to complete any punch-list item the buyer asked for prior to closing escrow.

Monica and my days were swamped with giant boards laying out the production phases of each property, including mile long lists of details we had yet to accomplish.

Chapter 12

Mark made some errors that cost our company dearly. By missing termite damage or a roof that had to be repaired, meant that we had to eat the costs. If unseen construction costs were not calculated in properly it could leave our company thousands short. Therefore, we began to collect construction bids whenever possible, prior to Mark accepting an offer on a new deal. This was the only way to ensure the contractors had tight requirements before beginning the project. But this also meant that my load increased substantially, as many projects were refused due to hidden costs that made it impossible to make money.

Mark still handled the bulk of estimates upfront but Monica and I stepped in when he needed more thorough bids. It seemed a relatively secure way to ensure we made money on the back end of the sale.

Mark would race to raise the money needed from investors with sufficient time to spare so we were not all sweating bullets to see if Mark could pull off the deal or not. It directly affected my job as the construction and design manager. I

wanted our construction teams to collect all bids from contractors, order termite reports or anything else pertinent to the
renovation of the property before we closed escrow. If our due
diligence was done prior to actually owning the property, then
construction could start immediately upon the close of escrow.
This way we were spending the previous owner's money while
we collected all bids, rather then waiting until after we closed
escrow, and the clock started ticking loudly on borrowed
money.

But on the other hand, I didn't want the crews wasting
their time estimating a project if Mark couldn't raise the money
to purchase the house. It was essential that Mark not only raise
the cash, but then communicated the details of the closing to
Monica and myself so we each could in turn direct our respective teams.

Mark was enthusiastic over my thousands of questions
to ensure I completely understood the new industry. Monica
and I peppered him continually on each aspect of construction
to minimize any errors. But whenever he ran short for funds,
I put in money. I happily contributed - it never occurred to me
to do otherwise.

Chapter 13

When we initially established our corporation, Mark insisted I become President and CEO, as it was my cash infusion that made the expansion possible. Mark suggested he take the Vice President and Secretary/Treasurer titles as he was handling the influx of investment capitol.

Early on Mark and I had a long conversation about the advantage of having woman-owned minority status. He believed that either loans through the small business administration or additional funding would be available if I was the majority stockholder. The era was pro-women, so it would help us advance through any financial crunch that all new companies experienced.

It wasn't until years later that the relevance of Mark's corporate positioning became apparent.

Chapter 14

Six months into the new company, I left for a week to meet MJ in Spain. Although we were twins, MJ remained a hippy while I chose a more conservative path. We were the same height yet had different facial features. We shared the identical voice, but my cadence was faster.

Like most siblings, we struggled through childhood tension and competition. It eventually fueled our need to find different paths at opposite ends of the country. She had returned to complete her education at the University of Pennsylvania, while I settled in San Diego. As we became adults we entered a difference phase, with both of us working to overcome the pain of our youth and reconnect. It took years and we became what twins should be – best friends.

MJ and I shared that mystical twin connection – feeling each other's pain or joy and often imparting thoughts. I missed her desperately and was ecstatic to see her in Madrid after she completed her language requirement for her degree.

We spoke several times a week but had not seen each other in over a year, as both our lives were too hectic to travel. We had planned this trip for eight months and were thrilled to have time together out of the country.

Although Mark and I were getting married the following month and we were working massive hours establishing our
new company, I felt the need to escape and relax in a different
culture with my twin sister. I had scheduled the trip with MJ
and just didn't want to cancel it.

I left the company and my cats in Mark's care. Mark
was supportive of the trip, as I hadn't had a moments rest
between closing my previous company and starting the new
corporation with him.

I flew to Spain with a deep sense of happiness over the
current state of my life.

Chapter 15

MJ and I spent a few days in Madrid then took a train to Sienna for the World's Fair. We loosely scheduled a day or two in Madrid, just kicking around playing tourist. The remainder of the trip would be spent in Seville, then to Portugal to enjoy the white sand beaches prior to flying back to the States.

Seville is the capital and largest city in the South of Spain. Many deem it one of Europe's most beautiful and charming cities. Legend states that it was founded by Hercules and enjoyed by the legendary figure, Don Juan.

The rich traditions of flamenco dancing, bullfighting and colorful fiestas all flourished in Seville. It was obvious from the first smell and texture of the city, that the people took tremendous pride in their history and traditions. The enchanting river ran through the city and provided an excellent boundary for the World Fair.

We had a wonderful time laughing our way through each experience. Toward the end of the week we spent a few days in Portugal. We enjoyed every element of our vacation, which included liberal use of my credit card. The vacation was my treat as MJ was a student with all the financial limitations that position represented.

Although I regularly used my credit cards, I was insistent about paying the balance in full each month. My credit limits were high, and when a card was declined after dinner one evening, it was a bit worrisome. I assumed it was a computer glitch and just used another. However, when my card was declined a second time, I panicked and decided to telephone the credit card company.

I couldn't get through on either the international number or the toll free number for the States, so I telephoned Mark and asked him to make a three-way call between himself, the credit card company and me. I proceeded to give the customer service representative my account, social security number, and mother's maiden name, and then waited while she researched the problem. It was a simple fix as my account was only put on hold until they verified the purchases in Europe to ensure they were authentic. Once the verification process was completed, the hold was released. I said goodbye to Mark and hung up, thinking my world was again intact.

MJ and I continued on our journey, unaware that Mark had used my credit card number in San Diego. Armed with my personal information, he proceeded to make purchases and take cash advances for thousands of dollars. I would not discover this for another full credit card cycle - well after we were married.

Chapter 16

The return flight from Spain was delayed making the trip much longer than expected. I arrived at 9:00 pm totally exhausted, but my spirits soared when I saw Mark waiting for me with flowers. We held up traffic departing the gangway while we embraced. I was overcome with a deep sense of love and found it hard to imagine what my life was like before I met him.

In the car Mark said, "I really missed you and I am so glad you are finally home."

"You made it hard to completely enjoy my trip!" I said it with a scolding tone, than I softened. "I do love you Mark."

"My world feels so empty without you. Don't go away again, ok?" He reached over and took my hand. The feel of him sent chills racing up and down my body.

I had felt the same sense of yearning, more than I thought possible. We arrived home to thrilled cries from my cats, who were equally as excited to have me back.

The house was filled with vases of beautiful flowers with several exquisite necklaces strategically placed among them. Candles of soft beckoning light surrounded the hot tub.

We shared moments of easy laughter in the warm water then retreated to the bedroom. The jetlag hit me hard and we slept wrapped in each other's arms.

Chapter 17

1 awoke early the next morning. My cats were still asleep, but thrilled their mom was up. They had a quick breakfast and dashed outside to see what had changed overnight. Mark had set up the coffeemaker to brew early, knowing that I would be up at the crack of dawn.

I began sorting the huge pile of mail on the breakfast bar. Most of the parcels were not urgent so I just put them aside to handle later. I hesitated at a card from my mother. I opened it and read the cryptic message twice.

Dear Alesandra,

Please call the second you receive this.
It's very important.

Love, Mom

Chicago was two hours ahead so I reached for the phone to call her. She picked it up with a rushed voice.

"Hi Mom, I just received your card. What's up?"

"Oh, Alesandra. Welcome back! How was your trip?"

"Great." I replied.

But before I could say anymore my mother spoke, "I received a telephone call while you were away. It... It upset me."

I felt my stomach drop.

"What, Mom?" I asked.

There was a moment of silence then she responded in what sounded like a hushed voice.

"Well, a woman called who would not identify herself. She told me that Mark was a crook. She said he has stolen money from people he was in business with and that..." Her voice trailed off.

"Mom?"

"Yes, I'm here." My heart was slamming in my chest.

She started again, "I received a call from a woman..."

"Who?" I cut in.

"She wouldn't say." My mother continued,

"She told me that Mark cheated people out of money... including her. She said that she had dated Mark for a time and that he stole her money. I really think you should reconsider..."

Something didn't feel right in this exchange. My mind was racing wildly. My mom would never have stayed on the phone with someone who refused to give their name. I did not hear whatever her last few words were.

"Mom, wait a minute," I interruped her. "How long did you talk to her?"

My mother was quiet and my suspicions were confirmed.

"You know who it is, don't you?" I said incredulously.

"Well, I promised her I wouldn't tell you."

"What? You have to tell me, I'm your daughter!" I felt betrayed.

My mother hesitated, "I can't."

By now Mark was awake and had entered the kitchen. He took at seat at the table and wiped the sleep from his eyes. Mark did not drink coffee but instead got up and retrieved a coke from the refrigerator. He sat down again and mouthed the words, *what's going on?* But I couldn't respond. I just put up my finger to indicate, just a moment.

I said again, slowly, into the phone, "Mom, tell me the truth. I want the whole story. Including who called you."

My mother finally said, "All I can tell you is that Mark can't be trusted. You should listen to me. Why don't you kids ever listen? I'm late for church. I'll call you when I get back."

With that she hung up. I disconnected the line and set the phone on the table. Mark was staring at me with a worried look on his face.

Chapter 18

"What's going on?" He asked now fully awake.

I looked at him with concern, "My mother received a call from a woman who claimed that you stole money from her and other people. She said you were a crook!" I gave him a hard questioning stare.

Mark got up from the table and nearly threw the chair back.

"It's Kathy, I'm sure of it!." He said in an angry voice.

"I didn't want to tell you anything because I thought she would just leave me alone... but clearly, that isn't going to happen."

"What are you talking about?" I was trying hard to control my temper.

"It's my ex. She keeps calling me. She said that she's finally getting a divorce and wants us to try again. I told her that you and I were getting married and that it was too late."

I looked at him, blank. My mind was still thick from the trip but sharpened by anger. The question was – *who was I angry at?*

The next couple of hours were spent discussing Mark's

relationship with Kathy. Much of it I already knew, but Mark went into greater detail.

He and Kathy had lived the high life, dinners, travel and social events, even though she was married. They had worked together at a large magazine in San Diego while Mark was working on establishing his real estate company. It was not uncommon to be each other's date well before the affair started. She began to invest in his new company and eventually he left the magazine to commit his time solely to his renovations.

Mark explained that they bought a couple of properties together that were still on the market. One was a rental. He painted her as a scorned ex-lover. A description I was more than willing to accept. Why wouldn't I? Mark had told me about their relationship early on, why would he lie?

He described in detail how Kathy was unhappy in her marriage. How her husband was grossly overweight and not interested in engaging in life, but rather, spent hours in front of the television.

Mark described Kathy as a sharp businesswoman. Their torrid affair lasted for years. She fell in lust and Mark fell in love. He asked Kathy to leave her husband on numerous occasions. She declined. Finally Kathy said she would leave, and Mark moved into a townhouse – a property they had bought together. He had dreams of building a life together. At the last minute Kathy had a change of heart and decided to stay in her marriage.

Mark had finally reached his limit and said he could not continue the relationship. Within six months he met me. We had been dating for quite a while when Kathy changed her mind. She decided to leave her husband, but Mark told her it was too late – that he was happy and that he wanted to marry me.

She retaliated by calling my mother, trying to drive a wedge in our link. He begged me not to let her animosity hurt us.

Chapter 19

By noon I was worn out, not sure who to believe, but leaning toward Mark. He secured the deal by offering to call Kathy on the speakerphone so that I could hear the conversation. We were at an impasse and I reluctantly agreed.

He dialed Kathy and started in.

"Kathy. What the hell do you think you're doing calling Alesandra's mother?" Mark barked into the phone.

"I thought they needed to know who you are!" Kathy wailed back.

"Yeah, your truth or the real truth!" Mark spit at her.

"Mark..." Kathy started, but Mark bit back,

"I waited years for you to leave Eugene. I even moved into the townhouse. We bought furniture together and then you never moved in."

Kathy broke in, "That's not exactly..."

"What? Are you saying you didn't change your mind? You knew I couldn't take it anymore." Mark softened, "I met Alesandra, fell in love and we're engaged. Can't you be happy for me? Do you hear me Kathy? Now, leave us alone!"

The line was silent for a minute, then Kathy spoke with a little less fervor, "Fine Mark. But you still owe me money!"

"Like hell. I'm trying to build a new life..."

Kathy was mad again, "How can you say that? You said..."

Mark didn't wait for her, "What!? I said we could do a couple of deals together. You wanted a way to make money separate from your husband. The properties are still on the market. When they sell, you'll make money, just like me!"

Kathy spoke very hesitantly, "Mark, what are you talking about? You said that..."

Mark cut in again, "That it's over? I've tried telling you so many times. You just won't listen. I'm warning you Kathy, if you don't leave us alone, I'll have to tell your husband a..."

"Don't even go there, Mark!" Kathy screamed.

"Then just leave us alone!"

Kathy spoke quickly, "Fine. I will."

Mark hung up and looked at me.

I was sitting on the couch all folded up. My legs were up on the edge, knees pulled in tight with my arms wrapped around them – clearly a self-protection pose. Mark knelt in front of me and put his hands on my knees, forcing my hands off. He gently lifted my ankles and placed my legs on the floor. He knelt close and leaned in.

"Alesandra, I'm sorry. I had no idea that Kathy would try to come between us like this. I mean, I knew she regretted her decision, but I thought she was over it." Mark looked deep into my eyes.

"I don't know what to think. I'm just humiliated that my mother was drawn into this. God, what do I say to her?"

"Tell her the truth. It was a scorned ex-girlfriend. That's all it is. Please don't let this separate us. I've told you all about my past. I'm ashamed I was involved with a married woman. I...just... Please?"

"I just don't know Mark." I was filled with confusion.

"You are my whole world. Don't let her come between us - that's exactly what she wants. I'll spend my life making you happy. Let me prove it to you."

He slowly got up and pulled me on my feet and into his arms. Gradually he guided me back through the house and toward the bedroom. He made love to me in the gentlest way and tenderly wiped any thought of Kathy from my mind.

Chapter 20

*H*alf-truths are far more convincing than outright lies. I was unprepared for Mark's trickery. He was a master at weaving his own truth with just enough accurate information to make it plausible. I realized much too late that Mark knew how to play on the doubts of women.

I expected him to deny the situation with Kathy in its entirety, but Mark was too smart for that. He agreed with just enough information to make the storyline believable. Then he denied significant facets – all the qualities that made Kathy look small.

I chomped on those tidbits – all to willing to believe. Mark wove a little teary emotion - a heartfelt whimper combined with just enough deniability. I was all too eager to believe that a woman was lying.

Chapter 21

Mark and I married one month later in an elegant ceremony at the Hotel Del Coronado's Duchess of Windsor Cottage. The cottage was a separate structure from the hotel itself, nestled in palm trees on a private segment of the beach. We chose the Duchess of Windsor Cottage since this quaint bungalow is where Edward, Prince of Wales, first met his wife who later became the Duchess of Windsor.

Mark and I strolled down the sidewalk bordering the beach from our hotel room to the back of the cottage. I had no awareness of my feet, but I did feel the warm salty breeze from the ocean brush against my bare shoulders. The sky was beginning to turn gorgeous shades of pink and soft yellow, flaunting the exquisite sunset yet to come.

The wedding took place in the enchanting cottage with two tall stone pillars marking the entrance that opened onto the private beach. There were two French doors where the Pastor held the ceremony.

We entered from the back of the wedding area off the beach, and walked up the center aisle to the steps of the Cottage. There was a long rice paper runner with two elegant floral arrangements in deep red at the base of the steps where the Pastor was standing. It gave Mark and I a target to shoot for as we were both floating by our guests.

I felt beautiful in my black velvet gown while Mark was the gallant looking groom.

The marriage began in fairy tale style and I wondered if it was all a dream. The wedding was at sunset on March 21, 1993, the perfect balance, as it was the Spring solstice. I prayed the metaphor of stability would be the foundation of our life together.

A few members of my family were present including my mom and younger brother Joe. MJ couldn't make the wedding as she had spent her vacation with me in Spain just a few weeks before. Between graduate school and a full time job in Philadelphia, there was no way she could come out for my special day. I was hurt but understood that she could not break from her studies.

After the ceremony, Mark and I drifted from guest to guest and exchanged words neither of us could remember. All I recalled was a loving feeling and a sense of pride. It left me feeling the future could only be radiant and successful. There did not seem a remote possibility that our marriage could fail when it began so perfectly.

Chapter 22

Mark and I couldn't take a honeymoon immediately as we were buried with the company, but it mattered little to either of us. Our life together felt rich and I was content to wait a few months before we escaped to an island to formally honor our wedding.

However, shortly after we were married Mark asked me to see a property he was purchasing for the company. We drove down a beautiful private drive bordering a national forest in an eastern community of San Diego. The house was a sprawling ranch style home that backed up to a large canyon.

Although from the street the home looked rather ordinary, the moment we opened the front door I squealed with delight. We walked through the open layout and I was mesmerized with the expanse of the home as well as the wide, vaulted ceilings. Most of the rooms were massive, but it was the back yard and gigantic deck that sprawled out over the canyon that won my heart.

I let the soft breeze fill my senses and just stood quiet, appreciating the beauty. Mark stood close and put his arm gently over my shoulders.

"What would you think about renovating this one for us?" He sounded a bit fearful to even ask.

"I can't imagine what this would cost Mark! But it is beautiful, my god." I felt a bit wistful, as this was the only property that had ever made me want to give up my home.

"Well, I can pick it up pretty cheap as it has a cracked slab. It may take a while to secure the financing, but I think I could arrange short-term money to carry us until you refinance." He spoke with pride.

"Me refinance? Why not both of us?" My internal alarm went off but it was muted instantly.

"Well, I still have so many properties in my name. We could probably get better financing if we just used your credit. I would really like a home that we shared together. I love your house but it does feel like I'm a guest. What do you think?" Mark nestled in closer.

"It's gorgeous, but I'm a bit nervous to increase the house payment."

I was tentative in my response, as I knew we were riddled in a high-risk business. I wanted to keep our personal bills to a minimum and we just had the expense of the wedding.

"Let me take care of it. I could rent out your home and not lose the equity you've built." He turned me toward him and kissed me deeply.

I held my new husband and then turned my body so my back was nestled into his chest. He held me and I looked out over the canyon. This gorgeous home was nestled in a grove of eucalyptus trees across from the Cleveland National Forest. The property was laden with nature and as the wind rustled up through the gorge, it gave me a deep sense of freedom.

The deck extended out over the valley and as the wind

blew, the grove of eucalyptus trees swayed in a private dance.

"OK Mark, handle it. I love it!" We stayed in each others arms staring out over our future.

Chapter 23

*T*he thought of a honeymoon was soon lost in the renovation of our new home. I poured money into the house and spent weeks deciding how to refurbish it.

Mark arranged investors for the cracked slab and short-term financing for the purchase, but my savings lovingly restored the house. I had a small crew that worked daily to prepare it for us. As the library and fireplace came to life, so did my desire to move. Although I would lose my pool, there was a perfect spot nestled on the edge of the canyon to install a large Jacuzzi tub. It was idyllic.

The master bedroom opened onto the deck and had a private pathway to the tub. We had an abundance of space and a rich slice of nature. As the day drew close to the move, my excitement began to climb. I was convinced that this new home would represent all the loving traits of our marriage and would provide a place where we could grow old together.

I remember a deep sense of joy the day we moved. As I drove into our new neighborhood, I was filled with excitement. This was my new home and I was married to a man I loved deeply. My life held such promise, yet there was a nagging sensation that something was wrong. I chalked it up to the startling increase in house payment that came with our dream home. I had signed all the loan docs and the reality hit me like a bolt of fear. Mark reassured me that we could easily afford the payment, as the company was growing at a rapid pace.

He handled the rental of my home. The new family would move in within one week of our vacancy. I held his need for fresh surroundings constant. Had I moved into his home, I would have felt the same way.

We arrived shortly before the movers and things moved at record speed. I set the cat carriers on the countertop in the kitchen – giving both cats a bird's eye view of the whole process. Selsie sang all morning. Zeff sneered but moved from the front to the back of the cage – clearly upset. I stopped every so often to express soft words of encouragement. I scratched their ears. One of the movers tried to reassure Selsie. She bit him.

Within four hours the furniture was in place and the movers gone. I was surprised how large and spacious the house felt. Even the dozens of boxes looked dwarfed in the vast open layout.

I placed the cat carriers on the floor in the family room and opened the doors. They inspected their new surroundings in a flurry, then headed for the open door to exit the house. They bounded out and darted across the grass to the edge of the canyon. Zeff and Selsie exchanged a look that said they hit the jackpot – then slipped over the edge. They returned before dark -- hunger brought them home.

Life couldn't be finer.

Chapter 24

About two months after the wedding my credit card statement came. There was a payment I had not made the month before as well as an ending balance much higher than anticipated. I called them immediately to inquire on the discrepancy and I was informed of multiple charges I did not authorize.

I requested the last two months statements be faxed to review. It reflected multiple charges from San Diego during the time I was in Europe with MJ. The statement also showed a payment the month before which I did not make. My heart was tight and I was reviewing it when Mark called me from his office asking that I meet with him.

I grabbed the paperwork, entered his office and stood across from his desk.

"Mark, this is odd. Look at my statement." I said it with a sense of dread thinking a stranger had my account information.

"Oh, sure. I had to use it while you were away and I made the payment last month so you wouldn't have to worry about it." He said it matter of fact.

"What do you mean? You..you opened my mail?" I sat down in one of the chairs across from his desk.

"Well sure. I knew it was my charge." He looked at me with loving eyes and my heart clenched in warning.

"But I never gave you my card!" I was shocked.

"Well, I knew we would be married soon and I ran short with you out of town." Then he saw the look of shock on my face.

"Are you saying you don't trust me? Great! We just got married and you think I'd steal from you?" Mark looked at me with contempt and sadness.

"I didn't say that, but I would never open your mail!" I was amazed that somehow this got turned around onto me.

Mark softened his look and said with the utmost gentleness, "*Please don't worry*. I'd never do anything to hurt you. I'll take care of it. We had some bills that had to be paid and I didn't want to burden you when you were out of town. I'm selling a property this week and I'll give you the money back."

Mark spoke smoothly but he could sense my amprehension. He came around his desk and sat in the chair next to mine. He reached for my hand but I pulled away from him. Mark was persistent and finally took it in his. He leaned close as if to reach into my soul.

"I promise you, there is nothing to worry about. I've got it handled. I know you are footing a large portion of the finances for the business. Doesn't that make us partners? I mean, we are married and own the company together. You have got to learn to trust me. I am not trying to manipulate you. What do I have to do to earn your complete trust?"

I thought of my two marriages and had to concede that my trust level had diminished significantly. Maybe this was how a real marriage operated. I really didn't know what a good partnership was so it was possible that my attitude had been jaded by past mistakes.

I didn't say a word but got up and left his office with a sick feeling flooding my body.

•   •   •

Mark paid me back in full as promised when the next property sold. I paid off my credit card, but within a few days he was asking for more money to float deals. It seemed like a never-ending river of cash that needed to be infused into the business, but I knew that the startup phase of any company was overwhelming. It generally took a few years to get in the black so I willingly poured in money.

My plans to return to college became a distant memory.

Chapter 25

Monica's and my pace picked up steam and before
I knew it we were working fourteen-hour days trying to keep
up with the flood of properties that Mark purchased, awaiting
renovation. We would tour the properties making lists of what
were the obvious changes. Then we would meet with the archi-
tect and contractors and set up a schedule for each.

We also had dozens of homes on the market after the
construction that wouldn't leave our division until after they
sold and closed escrow. We worked round the clock jamming
out plans and construction schedules.

Mark stayed focused on the investors, as that is where
his talent really shined. He was a man's man and admired by
anyone in his presence. Mark invited me to one of his presentations to potential investors. It amazed me how his broad smile
would open and his white teeth and dimples would light up the
room. Powerful men of all ages sought his attention. He would
stand with his stance wide and arms crossed as he held them
captive.

Women flaunted themselves in his presence, but Mark
only had eyes for me. He was often playing golf with a client

or in box seats at a sold out baseball or football game. His natural ease and athletic build permeated the investors and made them want to roll their money from one deal to the next.

I had always found men competitive with each other, but Mark had the innate ability to make each investor feel as if they were privileged to work with him. I would watch him operate, completely in awe of his talent. He was the life of the party, the investment group or the construction site. People just flocked to him and wanted his acceptance. His winning smile and full laugh only served to ingratiate himself. His lanky and muscular physique and glittering blue eyes could cut through any crowd. I have never seen one man who could move men and women alike and leave each person feeling as if they were graced to be part of his world.

Chapter 26

*T*he first year we renovated 57 properties and our business exploded. At our weekly meetings, Monica and I urged Mark to slow the growth, but he was adamant to force the vastness of the company. He laid out his plans and his eyes were wide with excitement over our rate of expansion.

Money was beginning to flow but I was overwhelmed with work. It was a never-ending river of properties, construction schedules and realtors. I longed for a day off but the company was growing too fast to even hire sufficient staff.

.   .   .

Mark and I fell into a rhythm both in the office and at home. Some days we barely saw each other but we always took time to have breakfast together.

I grew accustomed to our morning ritual. Mark would meet me on the deck with a tray of fresh brewed coffee, coca cola for himself and croissants. It became a custom that I adored – sitting on the deck watching the morning light fill the canyon while we planned our arduous day.

Chapter 27

The first signs of illness came through multiple urinary tract infections. I attributed it to a healthy sex life and just got the necessary medication.

Within a few weeks mild anxiety and irritability began to creep into my existence and I thought it was tied to the long hours we were working. I had a pervasive sense of nervousness and chronic headaches that would leave me dizzy. I also experiences bouts of low self-confidence and could not place the cause, but was too willing to attach it to long hours and little time for my marriage. There were many sleepless nights that I would toss and turn and eventually just got up.

But when bronchitis became a monthly affliction, I became more concerned. An ankle sprain on a construction site took me out of the office for a few days but healed quickly. It was not like me to be clumsy, particularly as I was familiar with construction zones through my years in engineering. It was as if a dark force was infiltrating my life leaving me prone to accidents and weakening my health.

A visit to my doctor provided a warning that I was

under too much stress and I needed to cut back my hours. I took the antibiotic for the bronchitis but felt his concern was a bit excessive.

·   ·   ·

Mark expressed alarm as well over the dark pillows developing under my eyes. He saw I was losing weight and asked if I needed more to eat. My appetite dwindled, making it difficult to finish a meal.

I knew my workload was tremendous, but I was used to long hours as I had a passion for work. In that way I was more like a man and always poured myself into my career.

This was different. It was as if my life force was beginning to drain out of me yet, I could not place the cause. I would have days where I felt relatively normal, then at others I was on the verge of passing out.

The weight loss was welcome, as I always felt better a bit thinner. But my clothes were beginning to bag as the headaches worsened. I didn't realize how much my looks had changed until MJ came for a weekend visit about eight months after I was married.

She took one look at me and her eyes got wide. After hugs and exclamations of how happy we were to see each other, we went for lunch. When the meal was served, she expressed her concern.

"Do you realize you're losing weight?" She asked with trepidation.

"Yeah, I know. I've been trying to shake these last five pounds for years and they finally came off." I said trying to minimize her concern.

"But you have dark circles under your eyes sis. What's

going on? Are you ok?"

"Oh sure. Just working crazy hours. I'm not sleeping as much as I should." I muttered hesitantly.

"You've been sick too much lately, first urinary tract infections, headaches, then bronchitis, how many times? Why do you think I came out to see you?" She looked hard at me, demanding an answer.

"Please don't worry sis. I've got a great doctor and I'm working to figure it out. I'll be fine, not to worry."

I dismissed the conversation and MJ knew it would serve no purpose to belabor the point.

We spent the weekend touring our properties and restaurant hopping across the city. It was wonderful to see MJ but she wore deep lines of concern on her face. Deep inside I knew why.

Chapter 28

After my auto accident at 19, I spent a few years filled with depression while undergoing surgeries. The depression and anxiety worsened, and I lost dramatic amounts of weight that eventually led to two hospitalizations where psychiatric drugs were used in an attempt to restore my mood. I remember the horrific side effects rather than any benefit from the medications.

The anti-psychotic and anti-depressant medications left me feeling numb to the world and I completely lost my willingness to engage life.

After the last hospitalization I moved to San Diego, and quit the drugs and suffered flu-like symptoms for a few weeks. It took years to get my life back on track and MJ was leery of anything that represented regression into the darkness. I was of a normal weight anyway and any weight loss or dark pillows under my eyes heightened her alarm.

This trip was the first time that any discord developed between MJ and Mark. I couldn't place the origination, as they always seemed to have a pretty good relationship. But this time the air was fraught with tension.

One night at dinner MJ asked Mark to pass the salt and he lifted the shaker and set it a few inches from his plate, then snickered. MJ bristled, stood and came over to his end of the table to collect the condiment. Mark laughed in an antagonistic way that made me narrow my eyes. We had heated words about his attitude later that night, but he told me that I was making more of it then was necessary.

The next morning I was walking down the hallway toward the kitchen and I heard snippets of an angry exchange between them.

"Why is this happening Mark?" MJ's voice was heavy with accusation.

"Sounds like you're blaming me!" Mark spoke with true vengeance.

"She wasn't sick when she met you." MJ spit the words at him.

"You're out of your mind!" Mark snorted.

I entered the room and they both stopped and just looked at me.

"What is wrong with you two? Please, stop!" I grabbed my coffee and headed outside. MJ followed.

"Sorry sis. I'm just worried about you." She was so tender.

"I know, but don't blame him, ok?" I pleaded with her. She just nodded with a look that belied her silence.

•   •   •

The remainder of MJ's trip, there was a slight edge between them as if they were both putting on airs. It left me very unsettled, as it was important to me that they get along. It brought back remnants of childhood jealousies that left me uneasy. I wanted her to be genuinely happy for me and not find fault in my husband. Regardless of how I tried, the air remained tense whenever they were in the same vicinity.

Mark sensed her distrust of him and expressed his sadness and anger over her coldness. Late night conversations were filled with his interpretation of MJ's behavior, including her jealousy or unresolved issues against me. He often expressed how *he wanted to be my best friend.* It left me feeling that MJ and I hadn't come as far as I originally thought. It saddened me. MJ in turn expressed deep resentment toward Mark and their interaction was stilted in distrust.

Mark's petulance contributed to my sense of unease as his attitude toward MJ had become increasingly intolerant. The last time he saw her they had actually joked a bit, although MJ was a bit aloof. This time they could not even tolerate each other's company.

Mark and I were having a disagreement the last morning of MJ's visit and unfortunately she witnessed his irritability. It began like any other day with Mark serving me coffee on the deck while we discussed updates for work. After my second cup of coffee he began to reprimand me on a paint selection on a property. The house sold instantly so his insult was unwarranted. Just as he finished his statement, MJ walked outside. Mark had never criticized construction options before and I was mortified that his first lapse would occur in front of her.

She boarded the plane later that afternoon with a deep worry line on her forehead.

Chapter 29

*I*n the winter of 1993, after two particularly hard bouts of bronchitis, my heart began experiencing serious arrhythmias. Again I sought the help of a general practitioner who prescribed more antibiotics and inhalers to help my lung passages dilate. I was also sent to a cardiologist who prescribed a beta-blocker to ease the irregular heartbeats.

My anxiety was increasing and had progressed into tiny electric sensations in my hands and feet. It became increasingly difficult to catch my breath, as if my lung capacity had diminished significantly. But it was primarily the insomnia that haunted me. Night after night I was completely exhausted and yet could not sleep more than an hour or two. It was the worst combination of bone weary fatigue and nervous energy.

Mark's attitude was deteriorating and he became progressively short-tempered with both Monica and myself. It seemed that any selection we made on a construction site upset him. I attributed it to stress but it wore thin as we were all overworked.

Meetings held criticisms for choices that were standards in our company. Monica and I rarely deviated from selections, as they had been proven successful and we were too busy to continually look for new products. Therefore, colors were chosen from a standard eight palette and appliances, marble, tile, etc all came from an assortment that we knew the public responded to. Mark was involved in the initial selections so his attitude was confusing.

He pressured me for money but I began limiting amounts as my personal funds were quickly draining. I asked him to provide reports outlining profit and losses from sales. He supplied two reports that were inaccurate and when I questioned the numbers, it created more tension between us.

Chapter 30

*I*n early 1994, Mark was still purchasing properties at an alarming rate and Monica and I had tremendous difficulty keeping the contractors on schedule. I asked Mark to stop buying any property until we caught up. He would agree and then leave a renovation budget on our desks for a new property he had closed escrow on.

Arguments ensued and the tenderness waned. Only morning coffee held any semblance to the early months of our marriage. Mark was often contrite and tender but it rarely remained more than an hour or two. The rest of the time was spent with tension brewing and an underlying current of anger. As my health deteriorated so did Mark's kindness. I felt deep resentment and anger from him and yet had no idea where it originated.

My lung capacity had diminished to the point where my doctor recommended I keep a tank of oxygen at home and at the office. I slipped the mask on whenever possible and allowed the clear gas to fill my lungs.

My intellect seemed to be diminishing daily along with my lung capacity. Short-term memory loss became a constant battle and I had to take thorough notes to remind myself of every detail. Along with increased nervousness were moments of full-blown panic. I would gasp for air convinced my world was shattering. Deep breathing the oxygen generally calmed me for a moment, but the panic returned in waves of terror.

My visits to the doctor revealed no clues, only continual doses of antibiotics and prescriptions for more oxygen and inhalers. The cardiologist performed multiple exams and diagnosed mitral valve prolapse. It was a common heart valve irregularity that affected millions of people without requiring medication. Apparently I wasn't that lucky.

Chapter 31

In June of 1994, MJ had completed her education in Philadelphia and moved to San Diego in the midst of my failing health. I had serious reservations about her moving to San Diego, as I knew she would be appalled at my physical state and blame Mark. But I also wanted my twin sister near me as I was feeling very overwhelmed and fearful over my physical condition.

Unfortunately, MJ was instantly at odds with Mark. There was no longer any pretenses between them and the additional tension wore thin.

I never attributed what was happening to me to Mark, but rather to the massive schedule we were keeping. He was short-tempered and my health was deteriorating – we each reacted differently to extreme stress.

• • •

By mid-summer my anxiety became even more pronounced and left a cloak of dread over my life. It was as if the tension in my body was changing the way I perceived light and sound. My eyes became sensitive to even indoor light and my sense of hearing was acute, perceiving tiny sounds as massive. My hand tremors were interfering with the tiniest of tasks but it was the overwhelming sense of dread that filled my days.

I was overcome with panic and trepidation over every decision I made, convinced I no longer had proper judgment or cognitive skills. My breathing was labored, both from diminished lung capacity but also from fear. Sleep was non-existent, and I would roam the house or work on my computer, anything to make the hours pass. I began to dread the quiet hours late at night.

I dropped more weight and within another few months I couldn't go more than a few minutes without reaching for the oxygen. The cool gas did not fill my lungs as it once had and it no longer felt as if I was receiving adequate air. The panic that gripped me was constant.

Chapter 32

I had days full of dizziness and mixed thoughts, but the first major seizure occurred at Horton Plaza, a landmark shopping center. It covers six city blocks and is a delightful mixture of open-air shops and restaurants. I used to love Horton Plaza and now the memory of the center holds too much pain.

Mark invited me to dinner and a movie one night, a kind act that I eagerly responded to. I invited MJ to join us as she was trying to stay as close to me as humanly possible. My hope was that more social situations would help ease the tension between them and maybe a truce would reign supreme.

We had been pushing extremely hard at the office and a night off was a welcome respite. I was bone tired and just couldn't clear my head all day. A good dinner was just what I needed but hunger was hard to hold onto.

We chose a cozy café and I gave my order to MJ while I secured a table. It was a coveted booth and I slid into the corner and waited. That is the last thing I remember until I awoke in the emergency room with concerned faces staring down at me.

The story was relayed by MJ and it terrified me. They came back to the booth with trays of food but I would not respond . My eyes were glazed and I was unresponsive to touch or words. MJ tried to encourage me out of the booth but I began to seize. Mark tried to grab me but MJ held him back. She ran for the phone and called the paramedics who arrived in moments. They slid me out of the booth and placed me on a gurney. A mouth guard protected my tongue from retracting down my throat.

The paramedics explained it was a seizure and began to lift the gurney into the ambulance. The shaking stopped and the guard was removed. Mark attempted to sit in the back of the ambulance with me.

I spoke for the first time and said "No! Stay away from me! I want MJ."

Then I went unconscious. The paramedics refused Mark entry and MJ made the journey.

I spent most of the night in the hospital but all testing did not reveal the root of the seizure. I was given medication and instructed to see a neurologist immediately. Then I was released.

Chapter 33

*T*he following day I awoke with an enormous head-
ache and my teeth hurt. I was perspiring heavily but my hands
and feet were ice cold. I had a fitful night and was completely
exhausted. My joints had swelled and extreme vertigo was
present. My teeth no longer felt as if they fit my jaw. I was confused and frightened.

MJ spent the night and was on the phone with the neurologist when I came into the kitchen. Mark was already gone
and I poured a cup of coffee. She looked up with concern and
told me we had an appointment in two hours. I felt short-tempered and didn't know why.

"Thank you," was all I said and I took my coffee outside to the deck to sit quiet.

MJ followed me out and looked like she was fighting
words.

"What?" My voice sounded tinny and distant.

"I think Mark is poisoning you." It was a challenge.

"Are you out of your mind?" I spat it at her.

I remembered times in our youth when jealousy arose
with boyfriends. My heart sank. Mark's claims that MJ was

jealous filtered into my tender brain.

"No, I think he is giving you something – I don't know what." Her eyes were focused on me and not blinking.

"You're crazy. He loves me! Please don't start. Can't you be happy for me? We're just going through a rough time. All marriages do." My voice sounded separate from me.

"No, I really think he is trying to kill you." She wouldn't waver and it really angered me.

"Why would you say something like that?" I was furious.

"I'm not kidding. You have to listen to me. Look at you! You're a bag of bones. You were healthy when you met him! It's been just over a year since you were married!"

"Don't talk like that!" I got up from my chair and stomped back inside to get ready.

My head felt like it would split. I brushed my teeth and as I rinsed out my mouth, I noticed my gums were bleeding profusely.

.   •   •

We left for the doctor's appointment with the air tense between us. MJ was tender but the morning exchange was still hanging between us. Eventually we drove in silence.

We spent the better part of the afternoon at the neurologist's office. He ordered a slew of testing and prescribed Neurontin, an anti-seizure medication. I was once again sent home to wait for the results.

Chapter 34

I had regular appointments with the neurologist over the next few weeks but all of Dr. Bakst's testing revealed no clues. Eventually the seizures were deemed of unknown nature. Although medically a root cause could not be determined, it was critical to control the seizures. Therefore, Dr. Bakst increased the Neurontin and we all prayed.

Neurontin made my body feel thick, as if I was living in someone else's skin that didn't quite fit. The headaches increased and I was nauseated without relief. My stomach began to bloat with my intestinal track feeling as if I had constant food poisoning.

•   •   •

Some days the seizures would consist of just blanking out without the ability to communicate. Too often the seizure activity would intensify at night and cause a release of my bowels and leave me humiliated.

I don't know what was worse, the seizures or the side effects of the Neurontin. My hands had constant tremors and my stomach was continually upset. The dizziness was over-whelming and I began to lose my hair. I was aging at a rapid rate and no longer recognized my reflection in the mirror.

Yet I was told that the Neurontin was minimizing the seizure activity and as horrid as the side effects were, it was important to stay on the drug. I complied, fearful of increased seizures.

Chapter 35

Although I knew my strength was fading daily, the increased anxiety and insomnia made staying at home impossible. Part of me refused to admit how sick I was and so I just kept trying to act as if I had a normal workday.

I would try to take additional time in the morning to relax on the deck, but my mind would race with all the unfinished projects waiting for me at the office. I would drag myself out of the house and carry myself through the day.

Monica was especially patient as I wasn't handling the bulk of the load as I used to. When we did tour the properties, she would always keep one eye on me. I tried to keep my misery to myself, but the seizures were common knowledge among the staff, as well as my diminishing lung capacity.

MJ called regularly, but became increasingly short-tempered that I hadn't quit working. She stopped coming over to the house, as she didn't want to see Mark.

My inner world shrunk as my terror increased over my unknown malady.

Chapter 36

I continued to work through it all and my relationship with MJ became more distant every week. Her conviction was steadfast and unbeknownst to me she took a sample of my coffee to a lab to have it tested for various poisons including arsenic. When it came back indicating that the poison was not present, she approached me to find other samples she could have tested.

My anger deepened, as I felt the negative test result should have stopped her suspicion. She continued to blame Mark and my temper repeatedly flared. We were at a standoff.

Mark rotated his cruelty at a rapid pace, shifting between nasty comments about my appearance and poor job performance. My memory was failing and I was making stupid mistakes yet I could not understand his bitter comments. There was no hint of his love or concern.

Mark's criticism was unbearable and yet somehow he would always seem to recover by preparing breakfast each morning for us. His tone was always subdued and his affect gentle. It never lasted long.

His persona evolved into a vicious demon that bore no resemblance to the man I married. I had an uneasy and illusive sense of danger lurking, but could never define it.

Mark seemed oblivious to my declining health. Who was this hostile man called my husband, who did not slightly resemble the man I fell in love with. What happened to him?

The communication between us held too much anger and I didn't like who I was becoming in this marriage. All the character traits that I associated with my darker side were surfacing, while the loving, kind, generous and compassionate woman was disappearing.

Chapter 37

I began to hear complaints of investors running short on properties. Mark never said anything about the Short Sales, but the word on the construction sites was that investors were questioning the job costs.

Each time I asked Mark, he simply said the investor rolled their money. I couldn't get a straight answer and the more I interrogated him, his disposition worsened.

I was entering his office one afternoon and uncharacteristically, his door was slightly ajar. I heard him discussing off-shore accounts. I opened the door and he quickly hung up the phone. I attempted to grill him on the conversation, but he held firm that it was an investor transferring money from the Caymans.

I left his office with a heavy heart. Mark's duplicitous response hung forcefully in the air, but the truth evaded me.

Chapter 38

My depression deepened in the fall of 1994, as the root of seizure activity was still not defined. Why couldn't they find the cause? I needed a name I could give my nemesis that would allow me the chance to defeat it. Without a title for my affliction, how would they ever fix me?

The weight continued to pour off of me and I went down past size 8 and below a 6. At size 4, I had lost over 30 pounds and I could barely lift my arms, as they felt stiff and full of lead. The seizures plagued me a few days a week.

My link to the cats became a tiny thread of memory. Selsie was devoted and sought me regularly but Zeff pulled away, unsure why I had changed.

The sleeplessness haunted me. No matter how deep my exhaustion, I would sleep fitfully and wake weary. I would drag myself through each day and fight to keep up with the volume of work. Each night I was convinced my body would fall into a deep slumber and yet I tossed and turned, unable to gain more than an hour or two of needed rest. My mind just wouldn't shut down and it left me full of dread. I was desperate for a solid night's sleep and could not understand how my brain stayed hyper-alert.

I suffered sleepless nights for another few weeks until desperation made me call my therapist.

I had seen Melissa in past years and really needed someone to talk to other than MJ and Mark. She suggested that I see a psychiatrist for my depression and sleepless nights. I heeded her advice and made an appointment with the referral she had provided.

Chapter 39

*D*r. Braun's office was on the upper floor of the Scripps Hospital complex in La Jolla, California. It exuded wealth, confidence and comfort. I waited with apprehension.

Dr. Braun opened the door to the lobby and extended his hand. He was a well-groomed, stiff man in his mid-thirties with a slight resemblance to Opie from the Andy Griffith show.

"I'm Dr. Braun, why don't you come back so we can talk."

I lifted out of my chair and followed him in a stupor. We walked a hallway of books and filing cabinets. He took me into an office with elegant furnishings - just my style. I started to relax.

Dr. Braun sat behind a large mahogany desk and motioned for me to take a chair across from him. The large glass window behind his desk revered the glory of the La Jolla coastline. It looked flat to me. I quickly scanned the room and felt at ease in the opulence. I settled in a chair and waited.

"Melissa filled me in on your situation. It's no wonder that you are having difficulty sleeping." He said in a soothing voice.

I nodded and the tears began to flow. I found another soul who understood, what a relief! He had blank pages in front of him and as I talked, he jotted down notes.

I blew my nose and whispered, "Yeah, it's been pretty hard."

Dr. Braun gave me a gentle smile. "Tell me how you are feeling."

"Well, I can't sleep. My mind just won't shut down. I'm incredibly weepy and my appetite is awful. These damn seizures are exhausting me and I just need to sleep."

I started to cry again.

He asked, "Do you feel hopeless?"

I nodded.

"Irritable?"

"Well, yeah! Of course I am irritable. My husband and sister aren't helping matters. They won't even *try* to get along!"

My temper flared.

"Are you fatigued?" He prompted.

"Yes, I'm exhausted. I already told you that!" I said a little too shrill.

"Do you have feelings of guilt Alesandra?" He said it in such a kind way that my anger rushed right out of me and I felt small.

I hesitated then answered in a small voice.

"Well, probably a bit. I mean, I think the worst things about Mark."

He jotted more notes. I was amazed how this man really knew me. Then he gave me my indictment.

"Alesandra, you have a *chemical imbalance* in your brain brought on by severe stress."

There it was, a chemical imbalance. It sounded so serious, yet now I had a term I could hang my symptoms on. He was still talking and in my reverie I had missed a few precious words.

"...the sadness, fear, overwhelming panic. It's all part of it."

He stopped and I jumped in.

"Can it be fixed?" I muttered.

"Absolutely, but it will take time." He pulled out a blank prescription pad and began to write a script.

"I'd like you to take this medication once a day, preferably at bedtime."

I was actually hopeful. This man seemed so certain.

"How long will it take to correct the imbalance?" I had stopped crying.

"Anti-depressants take weeks to build a blood level..."

"Anti-depressants?" I cut in. "Listen doctor, I remember taking them briefly a decade ago after my car accident. I felt awful. It was hard getting off of them and they made me feel numb." My anxiety was climbing.

"Well, those were Tricyclics and there is a whole new class of drugs called SSRI's that are very effective without the side-effects of the drugs in the past. I've had great success. I think they will help you through this agonizing time."

He spoke with such confidence. I liked this man. He was the expert. It certainly wasn't going well left to my own devices.

"Okay, but I can't wait weeks to sleep. What do I do in the meantime?" I asked.

"No, of course not. I'll give you something for sleep as well." He began writing another script.

"Why can't I just take the sleeping pill?" I asked like a small child.

"No, you have a chemical imbalance in your brain that

won't be corrected by just sleeping pills. It'll take a few weeks, but you'll feel much better." He spoke with an authority that made me feel a bit foolish for asking.

"Oh, do I need blood work for this? I remembered having to keep track of blood levels." I tried to regain my authority.

"No, these new drugs are different. It may take time to assess the ideal dosage for you, but we will figure it out. I'd like you to come back in another ten days." He closed his book and stood up.

"Okay. I'm on Neurontin for the seizures, will this interfere?"

"No, it'll be fine."

I made the return appointment and left his office with my prescriptions. In the hallway I glanced at my watch. Only thirty minutes had passed.

I drove straight to the drugstore and filled the prescriptions. I headed home confident that I found the answer. I slept for the first time that night.

I had no way of knowing that the nightmare had just begun.

•   •   •

With the new sleeping pills, anti-depressant and anti-seizure medications my sleep improved and the seizures began to decrease slightly. I went back to work with renewed conviction on the existing renovations. Yet my head felt thick, making it hard to concentrate.

My body was still rail thin but with the seizures decreasing, I began to feel that maybe we had the right combination of drugs.

Chapter 40

T he complaints increased from contractors that their invoices weren't being paid. Mark never said a word and was out of the office regularly, attempting to sell more Trust Deeds for properties. I would approach him when he returned, but my questions were treated as a mutiny. He would become incensed that anyone would dare defy his judgment.

I no longer had the energy to argue, as I knew it was futile. The man I married had disappeared. The imposter bore no resemblance to the once handsome and tender man. The beast lived full time in my home.

The money seemed to dry up over night and with it the construction funds diminished to a trickle. I was so numb that I couldn't negotiate thoughts around our precarious position.

I was always a woman of strategy, with the innate ability to maneuver in business. Yet I had lost any natural talent and could only look to Mark for a solution. Continual requests for money brought no bankable answers.

It had become impossible to concentrate, and I missed all the early signs of company failure. I had always had the gift of forecasting business and yet I couldn't even outline the costs on each project. The numbers just wouldn't calculate in my confused brain.

One night after work, Monica suggested we stay and try to determine exactly where the properties were financially and therefore what outstanding monies we could expect from the sales.

We worked tirelessly and the results were beginning to materialize. My stomach became tighter as the night wore on. We had all current project files dismantled and spread out on the conference table. The only documents I could not locate were the Trust Deeds showing what Mark actually raised on each property. Therefore I went into accounting and just did a tally of what was deposited by investors toward each property. The numbers held the truth.

Chapter 41

*I*t was right around sunrise that the magnitude of the situation was clearly felt. I lost my breath.

Of the seventeen properties in various stages of construction, most were going to lose money. The reasons were numerous and all pointed to one source – Mark.

He had miscalculated the construction costs, misjudged the predicted sales price of each house, misstated the costs to purchase the property or just flat out misrepresented the entire project. The numbers were staggering - $8,500 loss, $10,200 loss, $12,800 loss, $23,000 loss and the list continued to grow.

We were going to have shortfalls in the neighborhood of $280,000 and that did not include the office expense, payroll or what we needed to survive. My stomach constricted further. Monica and I did not speak - there was no reason. The numbers said it all.

The sun crested over the horizon but my world was black. I printed several copies of the spreadsheets and sat with my oxygen tank. I inhaled fresh gas and leaned my head back on my chair. I had to steel myself to deal with Mark. Where was I going to get the strength? Monica packed up her belongings and left to grab a few hours sleep.

I sat in my office staring at the art that one time brought me solace. I had to take the evidence home and attempt to talk to Mark. Just the thought of him sleeping soundly brought rage to my throat. He must have known. He dealt with these numbers every day, yet said nothing. He continued to present proformas based on lies and walked through the world without any hit of regret or concern for the lives he might ruin. What had I done?

I loaded my briefcase and slowly descended the staircase to my car. The drive home was a blur as there was no awareness of the car or road.

I turned onto my beautiful street and noticed that it had lost any appeal. The landscape looked flat, as if it was a temporary film stage that could be dismantled within minutes.

I pulled into the garage; saw Mark's car and my stomach constricted. Bile began to rise. I opened my car door and saw Selsie's little head through the cat door. Her eyes were wide. She saw me and ran through the opening. Zeff blew by me toward freedom. I reached down and scooped Selsie into my arms. Her little warm body was a tremendous comfort. I nestled my face in her fur and took a deep breath. I loved her smell. Tears rolled down my face. I set her down and headed for the bedroom.

Chapter 42

Mark was sound asleep, clueless. I noisily dropped my purse and keys on the dresser. He sat up in bed and began to say something. I cut him off.

"I've been working all night. I'll be in the family room. We need to talk." I turned and left with my briefcase.

Mark had set the coffee to brew early. I poured myself a cup and sat waiting for him.

Mark came in with a coke in hand. Without a word I opened my briefcase and handed him the spreadsheets. His face flashed with confusion then became angry as he scanned each page. About one third of the way through he stopped and looked up. His eyes were dark and his jaw was set. This was going to be ugly.

"What the hell is this?" He demanded.

I snapped. "What do you think it is? You said you knew this business. You said you had twenty years experience! How could you be so far off on your calculations?"

Mark just looked at me.

"What are we going to do Mark?" The tears rolled down my cheeks.

Mark stood and started to pace. He opened the curtains to let the sunlight in. When he turned around he was in complete control. He saw my tears and sat at my side.

"I really didn't know it was this bad. I knew we were running short on the construction funds but I had no idea we were going to lose this much money."

He spoke softer than I'd seen him before and then he stopped. I looked up waiting.

"Alesandra, you cannot expect me to know all the details on every property. I did the best I could. There were hidden costs."

I shot back, "Which I though you allowed for! This is a nightmare! I'm out of money. I have nothing left. My money is in half the properties that are going to lose money. It's in this house, the payroll and office furniture. Don't you get it – we're broke!"

My breathing became labored and I sat back down.

"We're out of business Mark. That's what I'm here to tell you. We're done!" The tears came back.

I was exhausted. Beyond mental and physical fatigue was the weight of what was coming.

"I just don't get it Mark. Where are the profits you projected? Where is the money you raised? Where are the Trust Deeds? I couldn't find them. Where…" I trailed off. I was deflated.

Mark got up and walked into the kitchen to retrieve another coke. He took a deep swallow and looked at me over the breakfast bar.

His eyes were bright as he said, "I know what to do, we'll ask Ron for the money."

My head reeled. This was not the response I expected. Ron Smith was our largest investor and would be heavily exposed by Mark's miscalculations. He was a shrewd investor and something about him frightened me.

"Are you out of your mind?" My voice had a heavy edge.

Mark sat down on the edge of the couch. He was clearly excited.

"Listen. No, it's perfect. If the properties go belly up he'll be out money on each. He'd invest, if only to protect his investments."

I felt light-headed. The last thing I anticipated was continuing the company. I didn't know what to make of Mark's suggestion.

"I don't know Mark. All it would do is prolong the inevitable."

Mark jumped in, "No really, listen. This could get you back your investment. We could stay in business. This would work. I'm sure of it."

I stood up and began pacing the room. I stopped into the kitchen to get another cup of coffee. Maybe the thick brew would help clear my head. I glanced outside and saw the cats harassing a lizard. My breathing started laboring again. I sat down with my back to the window. My eyes hurt. When did my eyes become so sensitive to the sunlight? I looked at Mark. His eyes were full of excitement.

Then Mark said, "Maybe Ron could get you some help. You could take some extra time to take care of your health."

This was the first time Mark showed any concern over my wellbeing since early on, but it did sound appealing. My face registered momentary indecision and Mark jumped on it.

"Listen Alesandra, I have dealt with Ron many times. I am absolutely positive that he will not just walk away. He's worth millions and I know exactly how to handle him."

He did have a point. If Ron declined, we wouldn't be any worse off. The idea of recovering my health as well as some of my personal investment *was* attractive.

Mark was the master of the deal and if anyone could convince Ron to invest with us, it was him. This was one of those rare moments when I prayed his magic would hold and that Ron would invest just enough to help us navigate out of this nightmare.

Mark always knew which buttons to push with me.

Chapter 43

Mark arranged a meeting later that day and insisted that I go to relay the construction costs. We drove together in silence, and entered the beach community of Bird Rock at 5:45 p.m. and casually drove down the narrow streets until we found the address.

Ron opened the door and invited us in. He led us into the living room where a large window revealed waves crashing against the beach. It was beautiful. My heart felt constricted.

I had met Ron Smith a couple of times in the office, but I did not have a sense of him other than the obvious. He was very wealthy and it showed.

Ron was much shorter than Mark and stood no more than 5'10". He wore skin-tight jeans and snug polo shirts with the collar open. His hair was closely cropped and he was a heavy smoker. His house reeked of cigarette smoke.

Ron sat in an overstuffed chair and we sat facing him on the couch. It felt much like a king holding court. My heart palpitations increased in earnest. Images of being beheaded flashed briefly.

A skinny blond woman was asked to leave the room.

She complied without comment. The rules were established.

The next two hours were spent with Mark pitching another deal. This time it was our company and my future.

I was amazed at the skill Mark used to pilot his presentation. He knew exactly what to say, how to withdraw and when to stop talking. I thought for a moment that he was losing Ron as he was furious initially, but as Mark continued the dance, Ron's interest piqued.

By the end of the meeting he agreed to infuse up to $300,000 over the next few weeks, as long as he could control the spending. He would then reassess the situation and decide if any additional funds would be extended. Mark was pushing for two million but the $300,000 would cover us temporarily, provided no additional mistakes occurred.

Mark readily agreed. I nodded my ascent.

Chapter 44

$\mathcal{R}$on's infusion of cash allowed the inevitable to extend a few more months, but eventually he refused to risk any more capital on a dying venture.

As the funds dwindled, Mark's abuse escalated. He began openly kicking holes in the walls and breaking telephones. His verbal assaults on the staff increased and they began to quit. No one wanted to take his insults.

Yet each time an investor came into the office, Mark could turn on the charm and go straight into his pitch. It was odd to watch how quickly his persona would change. He could be in a full-blown rage, sadistically ragging on a staff member, then turn on a dime and greet an investor with total sincerity. Mark never looked back to see the trail of destruction.

Investors called the office or made unannounced visits trying to determine the status of their Trust Deeds. My heart broke for them, as I knew we would all lose our investments. Like myself, they placed their trust in Mark. It was all smoke and mirrors.

But I was the President of the corporation and felt like I had let them all down. The guilt ate at my soul and I wondered how I would ever forgive myself.

Chapter 45

*I*t was a mistake trusting my husband, but I realized it much too late. I was appalled with myself. My finances were gone and with them any thought of leaving Mark was quickly dismissed. Where would I go? How would I start over with my health in such a state of decline?

I had held the slim hope that if I could recover a small portion of my money, it would provide a nest egg to move to a tiny apartment and heal. But even that dream faded as the money evaporated. I felt powerless and boxed in at every turn.

I rifled through the files and saw hundreds of Trust Deeds for properties floating through the office. Mark never produced all the missing documents, but even the ones that remained gave a clear picture of the amount of money he had raised. They represented millions of dollars and the thought continually filtered in, *what has he done – where is all the money?*

Did he hide the money? But how could he if they were secured by the property? Were there properties I didn't know about? That didn't make sense either as escrow was in close touch with Tina and Lora.

My mind was too thick to piece together the nagging details. Something was terribly wrong but my brain was too foggy to make sense of the erroneous state of our company.

All I knew was that the conclusion was drawing near and I had no idea what that meant.

Chapter 46

Mark's volatility was erupting wildly and left all our nerves frayed. I also had Ron's pent up anger to diffuse as he was trying to protect his vulnerable investments.

Ron insisted on meetings each morning and it was becoming increasingly difficult for me to arrive on time. I saw no reason to meet daily for a dying venture. Yet Ron was convinced that if he kept the stream of properties coming into the company, he could somehow contain the losses Mark created.

Ron made unreasonable demands on production schedules and began to put undo stress on construction crews. The foremen would complain and ask Monica and myself to keep him off the site. They were moving as quickly as humanly possible and did not need his attitude.

The stress continued to spiral out of control. Although the antidepressant numbed my body, my sleep continued to deteriorate, even with the sleeping pills and once again, the seizure activity increased.

I was hanging by a thread.

Chapter 47

My marriage was unbearable and my loneliness was at such a deep level, as the one person I needed was my husband, and he was abusive.

I remembered how Mark flew to New York and insisted I rest. I thought of the lovely way he used to start each morning and the string of kindness he would extend throughout the day. All the nuggets of humanity ceased long ago. He even refused to feed the cats or turn on the faucet for Selsie.

Selsie retaliated by peeing in the sink in his bathroom. She held the same contempt I did.

The only ritual he maintained was to deliver my morning coffee, but his face always belied a cruel monster lurking. I often let it go cold.

•   •   •

I have never been a lonely woman, but rather relished my private time. This was a different type of loneliness, however. It was a desperate need for a partner to help me endure the fear surrounding me.

Lonely cannot describe the depth of pain my body and mind were suffering. I began to view the world as a site full of anguish.

My body was riddled with guilt over the losses facing our investors. Many I had never met but I saw the names cataloged in reports. The forenames were from decades past, and it told me how old they were. I wondered who had invested their life savings with Mark. What would happen to them? Were they ill like I was or were they oblivious to the threat?

My body felt like it was stuffed into another skin with no relationship to myself. I would stare in the mirror hoping to recognize just a tiny fragment of the passionate woman that used to exist. What gazed back was an obscure body, now emaciated from medications with deep-set eyes that were hollow. I was ugly.

My hair looked like straw and my eyes were not soft, but rather pinpoints glaring through my reflection. Who was this woman? Where did I go? The replica facing me in the mirror frightened me, as she bore no resemblance to my memory.

My personal grooming used to be performed with inordinate care. I enjoyed applying my makeup and fixing my hair. Now I raced through the process so not to face my portrait.

Mark had driven such a deep gulf between MJ and myself that I couldn't call her – I wouldn't know what to say.

I also had no inclination to see any of my friends. Had it not been for my little cats, my thoughts of suicide would have certainly been answered.

Chapter 48

*A*nd yet I continued working through all the insanity. I had the foolish belief that somehow I could protect the investors. I knew my fortune was lost forever. I toured the properties, reviewed the contracts for ways to cut costs and tried to keep the existing projects on target. I wanted as many of the investors as possible to recover their money and run like hell. I knew I had nowhere to hide.

But with each day that passed, I was overcome with the tenuous state of both my health and the corporation's finances. A budding thought began to take form but I fought it off as it meant an irrevocable decision I just wasn't ready to face.

My load was not only massive — it was inhuman. My hours increased from one hundred plus hours a week to nearly one hundred fifty. I was at the breaking point and it came one afternoon as I looked around the office and knew my world had somehow shifted. Nothing looked the same. I wasn't sure what was happening to me but I just didn't feel anything. The totality of my experience was similar to being on acid, but without any hallucinations. I didn't feel of this world or separate. I packed up my belongings and began to walk out the door.

Monica caught me just as I was leaving.

"I got the list from escrow and three deals fell out. The properties didn't sell." She spoke hesitantly.

Finally the verdict snapped inside my being. I just smiled, shook my head and answered, "Thanks."

Somehow it all made sense but I didn't want to act rashly. I never left the building and instead returned to my domain. I looked around the office and realized it was all an illusion. It had been for a very long time.

The remainder of the day passed without incident. I did not engage conversation nor was I difficult. It was all said. I just needed time to think. My mind was too full as it was.

I had some decisions to make.

Chapter 49

I arrived home to find a note from Mark that he would in late. He was staying out with more frequency, claiming he was raising money. I suspected he was preparing his exit strategy.

I looked around the house and felt the cloak of reality close in. It all looked so welcoming, so lovely, that it belied the ugliness.

I poured a large glass of water and joined the cats on the patio. The warm air was peaceful, another sign of the lie. I stood on the deck and watched the world of nature. It seemed unaware of what was coming. How I wished I could live like that again.

It all looked flat. I wondered when the colors, sounds and sensations of the canyons that used to warm my heart, had mutated into images that held no reality. I had lost my precious link to nature.

The cats rubbed against my legs, calling me to attention. I sat down and stroked them numbly. They knew- they always knew what was happening with me. Selsie reached for me, as she needed the comfort. I gathered her into my arms and held her close, breathing in the scent of her. It did not alleviate my torment.

I sat there plotting. I felt it was time to end the charade and make one final measure to sell the properties. If it failed then it would be finished. But I also knew that it had terminated long ago, I just refused to accept it.

As my resolve grew in strength, so did my exhaustion. My body hurt. My head was thick yet full of lucidity. The fading sun grew warm and I shifted my position. The world around me was peaceful, but not for long.

I went into the house and took a look around. I did not turn on the lights. My decisions required shadows. I left the cats with their dinner and stripped off my clothes. My reflection reminded me of the dangerous state of my health. I looked more like a concentration camp survivor. It would be revered in Hollywood. I knew better.

I pushed my bedroom door open and padded to the hot tub. The jets bubbled up. I slid my body into the water and laid my head back. The night air was quiet. The canyons were dark. I turned off the jets and let the silence envelop me. I needed my decision to settle in the quiet.

I knew in my heart that my pronouncement was long overdue, but the guilt was nagging at every fiber within me. I felt as if I failed everyone. Could I live with my verdict or would I always blame myself for making a choice that affected so many?

In the distance I could hear the phone ringing. It didn't have the sting of the past. My world had shifted. I went inside and showered. Normally it relaxed me. Tonight it only served to sharpen my resolve.

I stepped out to dry off and the room became hazy. The edges grew fuzzy and it all happened quickly - another seizure.

I awoke naked, on the floor. The cats were licking me. I felt nauseous. I stumbled into the bedroom and sat on the edge of the bed. My head felt like it had been knifed. The red dials on the clock felt piercing. It was 1:18 am.

I didn't know if Mark was home and suspected that even if he were, he would have left me without assistance. I closed my eyes but the room started to spin. My head was thick with confusion and fear. What was happening to me? I lost consciousness before I could explore that thought.

Chapter 50

*T*he clock showed 3:20 am. The house was dark and the cats were next to me. They cried with relief as I got up. I was so cold. I wrapped myself in a warm robe and held up the walls as I made my way to the kitchen. I needed water. I poured and drank three glasses quickly. Much of it escaped down the front of my robe.

I leaned against the countertop and tried to support my body. The weakness was overwhelming. My body needed nourishment but it was too gigantic an effort. Water would have to suffice.

I slowly walked the house. Mark still wasn't home. The machine was flashing loudly. I hit the button. MJ's rich voice filled the room.

"Alesandra, I really need to talk to you. Please call me! I don't care what time it is. I need to talk to you tonight!"

Great. I had put tremendous distance in my relationship with MJ, and I just couldn't take another conversation full of accusations. She detested Mark and was convinced he was this master criminal. My heart was full of a completely different reality. It wasn't so important to me anymore where the fault lie, I mostly blamed myself anyway. Right now it was more important to make some changes. I needed a new life.

I padded back to the bedroom and crawled into bed. My body needed a few hours sleep. At 7:00 am I slowly pealed back the covers so my head was exposed and contemplated the day with a strong determination.

Mark entered the room with a cup of coffee. He looked a little sheepish, as he did most mornings. The coffee was his way of apologizing and it grew tiresome.

"Where were you all night Mark?" It was said without jealousy, just a flat question.

"I got in late. You must have been asleep." He never missed a beat and could lie without conscience.

I didn't bother telling him that I was awake. It would accomplish nothing.

I took the cup of hot steamy liquid and sipped it. MJ's warnings echoed just as it slid down my throat. I looked at it suspiciously and set it on the nightstand.

"I know you like your coffee hot. If it sits it will get cold." Mark said.

"In a minute. What time are you going in today?" I asked.

I wanted to get out of bed but I didn't want him to see me naked. We no longer had that connection. I couldn't re-member when we last slept together.

He had moved to the guest room long ago. I never ques-tioned him and felt grateful for the reprieve. He disgusted me and I questioned how I could have ever found him attractive.

I suspected Mark must have been having an affair, as he was a highly sexed man and had not suggested making love in longer than I could remember. I was indebted to whoever the poor woman was. At least she kept him from trying to approach me.

"Soon. I'll be there most of the day." Mark spoke a little too guarded. "Why?"

"I'm calling a meeting, but it won't be until this afternoon. I've got a couple doctors appointments this morning. I won't be in the management meeting. I'll leave a message for Ron. Could you leave so I can get ready?" My voice was tight.

He backed off and handed me my coffee.

"Finish that cup and I'll get you another while you are getting ready." Mark turned and left the room.

I hesitated and then felt foolish. I sipped the dark liquid, hoping for energy.

I got up and showered. Mark was gone when I came out of my room. Just as well, what I needed to say had to be addressed to the whole group.

My conviction fed energy into my bloodstream. This was a pivotal day.

Chapter 51

I drove to my neurologist's office for my 9:00 am appointment. I was led to an examining room where I tried to read a magazine. My mind wouldn't work - it was always confused after a seizure.

Dr. Bakst entered with a concerned look on his face. He had test results and other documents in his hands. He sat across from me and started in.

"All the tests have come in. I don't know how many more we can do as we keep running them and nothing is showing up. Most are within normal limits but your white-cell count is very high. I'd expect that with the reoccurring bronchitis. Hmm, I see you have lost more weight. Did you bring the journal?" Dr. Bakst looked concerned.

I handed him the record of seizure activity for the last two weeks.

"It has gotten worse. You really should quit working." He mumbled. I didn't say a word and waited.

"The MRI came back clean. I suspect that you've been experiencing quite a bit of dizziness and confusion with this level of seizure activity." He put the paperwork down and looked at me.

"It's getting worse. I just have a muddy mind. Figures, conversations, they are all starting to run together. It's as if I can't get the thoughts to actually come out of my mouth. Like there is a delay in the circuitry. Sometimes it feels dreamlike. Is that normal? I mean, normal for what's happening to me?" I had so many questions but couldn't phrase them.

"Well, seizures are caused by abnormal discharges of electricity in the brain. The symptoms you are describing are common. We have checked for neurological abnormalities, infection and any toxin in your blood. Everything is indicating normal levels. You are under an inordinate amount of stress and that is certainly a factor. You need to quit working." He was in doctor mode and on very comfortable ground.

"Toxin?" My mind stuck on the word.

"Any unusual element." He looked at me puzzled.

"Did you test for anything?" My mouth was instantly dry.

"Of course. We always test for a battery of toxic elements when there is not any other explanation for seizure activity." His face was full of questions.

"Nothing showed up?" I said desperately needing some water.

"No, of course not. As I said, your blood panel is within normal limits, excluding your white-cell count." He dropped his head back to the papers in my file.

I felt a bit foolish. MJ's fear was touching but clearly unwarranted.

"Alesandra, it's time for you to quit work. I mean it. We have tested for everything possible and the only conclusion I can make is that your seizure activity is directly tied to the amount of stress you are under. I've never seen anything quite like your condition, but this *will* kill you if we do not handle it now. You said you would slow your schedule but if anything, it's getting worse. I insist you stop working and take care of yourself. I'm drafting a letter to the State disability office. You need rest." He was very firm and left me no other options.

I started to say something but he put up his hand.

"No, it's time. You must focus on your health. Business can wait. Your life is at stake. I'm switching you from Neurontin to Depakote. We have to try something else."

He reached out and touched my shoulder lightly. It was as close to a hug as the good doctor came.

I nodded my assent and said, "I agree doctor."

I got up to leave. He had no idea how much I concurred with his assessment.

Chapter 52

My next appointment was with Dr. Braun. He went over the list of antidepressants he had tried without success – Wellbutrin, Paxil and Prozac.

"The only one you seem to tolerate is Effexor. I'm increasing the dosage to several times a day."

"I'm not sure about this doctor. My depression isn't any better and these drugs have so many side effects. Between the constipation, dry mouth and nausea, I'm miserable. Why can't I just take something to help me sleep?"

I was taking five different drugs including Neurontin, Restoril, Sinequan, Effexor and Klonopin and the cocktail made me feel awful. It was impossible to differentiate the side effects from the original complaints. But I also didn't know what was the symptom of seizures or what was the depression.

"The treatment of depression is trying to find equilibrium. Once we compensate for your chemical imbalance, you will feel substantially better. It takes awhile to build the proper blood levels. I'm convinced the side effects are coming from the Neurontin, but certainly not from the medications I'm prescribing. A dry mouth is the most common and annoying side-effect, but just keep a bottle of water with you at all times. I think you seem much better. Your attitude is more positive and your depression is lifting. You were crying during your last visit. It may be hard for you to assess improvement as you are seeking perfection. That may not be attainable with your marriage where it is. I'm going to increase the anti-anxiety drugs as well. You should be much calmer in no time. Please come back in another ten days." Dr. Braun stood up and walked me to the door.

I had my prescriptions in hand and left the building. It was nearly noon.

Chapter 53

The drive to the office was slow. I had to prepare for what was coming. I had called Ron and asked to meet the team just after lunch.

I arrived to find the office in a state of bedlam. Everyone was racing around putting out fires.

"Please call the team and ask them to meet me in the conference room."

I scooted away before Tina could ask any questions. I slipped into my office and gathered my pile of messages.

The team was milling in the conference room with familiar degrees of anger across their faces. Ron looked up and started in.

"You miss the morning meeting then call an emergency session?" He was enraged.

"Everyone sit down. I have some things to say." I was calm. They took their seats.

I gathered my courage and started in, "I can't go on like this anymore."

Ron looked up and Mark began to speak. I just held up my hand with the palm open.

118

"No, I mean it! I just came from my doctor's and it isn't good. The details aren't important, but this is what's going to happen. We are going to auction off all remaining properties. I have a report from the accountant that outlines the monies against each. I want the auction to be held in two weeks. If anyone disagrees or tries to block my decision, I'll file for bankruptcy immediately." I waited for the eruption.

Ron was the first to speak. "Actually I think it's a great idea. We can clear our pipeline." His comment surprised me.

Mark jumped in, "I think we should just file bankruptcy now. Why wait?"

I wanted to throw my chair across the room at him.

"No. You can't file without me and I'm not willing to do it without first attempting the auction. I feel an obligation to at least try and get all the money back to the investors. They trusted us and we have a responsibility to all of them!" I turned away from Mark.

"Any other comments?"

We spent two hours hashing out details. It was the most productive meeting ever held in our conference room. Just before the meeting ended I made the final comment.

"Ron, I don't want to purchase any new properties until we see whether the auction is successful. If it fails then I am closing the company." I said it with as much bravado as I could muster.

"What?" Ron spit it out. Everyone else remained quiet.

"You heard me. I can't do this anymore. If the auction is successful and we get the investors their money back, then I want to scale everything down to a pace that is much more manageable. If not, I'm shutting it down." I waited, grateful I was not seated next to him.

My heart was thumping so loudly I was sure the room could hear it. He stood up and said in a thin voice,

"Let's work on the auction." With that he left.

Chapter 54

The next two weeks were spent in a rush of activity getting everything ready for the auction. The properties were photographed and completed if at all possible. Even those in early states of renovation were cleaned and made presentable. The office was focused on a target auction date and it kept everyone's eye on a single goal.

As the date approached, Mark's nervousness increased. He continually undermined our efforts and pushed instead for bankruptcy. He went to the job sites and asked the crews to stop the construction but they took their orders from Monica and myself and refused him.

Mark brought court documents to the office one afternoon and tried to get me to sign them. I saw the words *Chapter 7* and asked him to leave. He then refused to even come into the office and participate in any effort to save the company or pursue the projects he was handling. We all ignored him and just kept our focus fervent.

I was fighting for the investors and the staff was seeking continued employment. We all had our end goal and it held us together toward a common objective.

I couldn't understand why he wanted the company insolvent but tried to stay focused on the task at hand and avoid him. I wouldn't engage him and instead stayed on point.

On night about ten days from the auction, I arrived home to find Mark waiting for me. He had a pile of papers strewn across the kitchen counter. I came in and he looked up and smiled. I bristled and tried to steel myself for whatever he was seeking.

"I've been reviewing the auction numbers and I'd like you to see them." He was trying to be the temperate man, but I had seen the monster too many times to trust this phantom.

"Why, Ron has already secured all the costs involved?" I was wary and kept my distance.

"He may not have these." Mark's eyes narrowed slightly.

I walked hesitantly toward the counter and picked up the spreadsheets. I could smell his cologne and my stomach turned. I captured the sheet and walked to a safe distance. Column after column outlined the properties. My eyes followed the list down until I hit the bottom line - all in red.

"If you go to auction you will have to come up with the money to close escrow. We don't have it. Why not file bankruptcy? It's the only way." He looked smug.

I knew many of the properties were in the hole but a few looked flagrantly off. The construction costs were inflated as well as the interest costs to ensure a loss. He was all about slight of hand and this was no different. He was pitching me.

"Well, Ron has accounted for the losses. The investors have agreed to take Short Sales if necessary. Its better than getting nothing." I tried to not show that I could see his falsities.

Mark jumped up and raced toward me. He tried to

snatch the spreadsheet out of my hands but I turned in time and he reached for air.

"I'd like to review this though and make sure our costs are accurate." I turned to leave the room quickly.

Mark charged me and literally slammed his body into me. I flew backward and hit the edge of the dining table. I felt my back pop loudly as my hip jammed into the table. I let out a startled shriek then dropped the pages to keep my balance. It didn't help as I tumbled to the floor.

He scooped them in mid-air and left me there.

"You're a fool. All of you are!" Then he left the house and a moment later I heard his car screech out of the driveway.

I rolled on my side and tried to keep the excruciating pain at bay. The cats found me there and Selsie licked the tears from my face. I slowly picked myself up and headed to the freezer for ice packs. My back and hip felt as if a car had hit me.

I knew it was far more sinister.

Chapter 55

I nursed my injuries but something in my spine felt as if it shattered. I pushed the pain away and iced as often as physically possible.

Mark stayed away for the next few days and I was grateful for the reprieve. I hated this man and yet did not know how to extricate myself from his clutch.

•   •   •

Finally all the advertising was formalized. The local realtors were notified of the auction and many confirmed attendance. Brochures were printed and the marketing blitz informed any potential buyers. I felt hopeful for the first time in spite of my deteriorating health. I only wanted to clear the pipeline enough so that many investors were repaid and the company could remain, albeit a smaller version. I felt the weight of the world on my shoulders.

As the auction date drew near my nervousness increased. I could feel something was amiss but all the details appeared to have been completed. We had nothing to do but wait which has never been one of my virtues. I am a woman of action. Having to sit idle while the winds of fate blow was pure agony.

Mark eventually came home with flowers and a deep apology. I left them on the counter until they wilted. His chagrin façade hung longer than usual but I no longer believed him.

I could hear him whistling in the shower and it made my nerves heighten. I locked my bedroom door at night, unsure of when the beast would hurt me again. Selsie, Zeff and I stayed barricaded in through the late night hours, but it mattered little, as Mark rarely came home until morning.

He was contrite and wanted to talk over morning coffee, but that had long ago lost its charm. I preferred to sip in silence. I no longer knew this stranger and vowed to leave the imposter as soon as possible.

Chapter 56

The morning of the auction I awoke at 3:15 a.m. dripping with sweat and trembling violently from a nightmare. The memory was at the forefront of my mind, but just out of grasp.

Mark was sleeping soundly in the guest room, completely oblivious to my panic. He chose to come home a few hours earlier and I could hear him banging around in the kitchen. I burrowed further into my covers and closer to the cats, pretending they were an army protecting me.

Mark and I had grown so far apart that we no longer shared that mysterious connection that allowed us to intuitively know the other's thoughts. It was hard to believe that it ever existed.

I used to love this man in a way that made me value him more than myself. I cherished his laugh, tender touch and smile. A whiff of his cologne would make my knees weak. Now I was revolted by the thought. I imagined that this was what a soldier felt prior to going into battle - the tingly fear of knowing that your adversary was trying to harm you. Now I knew that self-preservation was of utmost importance.

Thinking of Mark sleeping made me realize the travesty

of our marriage. I went into the bathroom to wet down a cool washcloth. I began wiping the fear off my face as I walked the long hallway to the kitchen.

I reached the refrigerator and drank directly from a large bottle of cold water. Although my thirst was overwhelming, I couldn't get the water down my throat fast enough. It was a strange, simultaneous sensation of absolute dehydration and overwhelming suffocation. The water was pouring into my mouth faster than I could swallow, leaving the excess to escape and run down my unclad emaciated body. I guzzled half the bottle.

What was I dreaming? Considering the magnitude of the day facing me, it was apropos that it began in terror. In a few short hours the destiny of the company, the means of many investors and my personal providence would be determined. Either we would come away from the auction with sufficient equity to pay off our debt, allowing the company to remain open or the antithesis would be confronting me with all its consequences.

Strange, up until this point I refused to contemplate what insolvency of the company meant. Would it leave me destitute? Where would I move? What would my life look like? The thought now horrified me. As much as I wanted my freedom from Mark, I knew that my health made it impossible to gain employment. If we lost the company, then my home would be lost as well as my car. Is this what happened to the masses who roamed our streets homeless? Would that same fate befall me?

I stood in the shower trying to imagine the days when the water sliced off my skin and felt rejuvenating. Now it hurt and left me feeling weak. I glanced down and saw the massive bruise across my hip and felt the throbbing in my back and knew unequivocally that my days of simple innocence were over. Who I would be after the whole scenario played out was still unclear. But the realization filled me with overwhelming grief. The shower couldn't cascade enough water to wash the tears as they fell. I was drained before I dressed and the magnitude of the upcoming event was weighing heavily. I felt as if a thousand pound burden was being carried on my thin frame.

I left for the auction completely detached from reality. My body was in a state of depersonalization, unable to feel the ground beneath my feet, and powerless to determine the temperature of the outside air. Every morsel of energy I mustered for the auction flattened before it even began.

The entire staff, excluding Mark, had labored tirelessly on a dire attempt to secure their employment.

Chapter 57

1 arrived several hours early, praying for a full house and active bidding. Monica was setting up the registration area. She looked up with surprise.

"What are you doing here? I thought I told you to sleep in and leave the setup to us." She was a bit cranky.

"I planned on it but couldn't sleep anyway." I stood blankly looking around.

Monica had empathy written all over her face.

"I couldn't sleep either. I... I don't know what to say."

Monica looked haggard. She was frighteningly thin and her language had diminished the last few weeks as well.

"Are you okay Monica?" I asked with concern.

She wasn't tracking well but I attributed it to the level of panic we were all experiencing. Monica nodded and went back to work.

I turned and headed toward the podium. The auctioneer was setting up the microphone. We spoke for a few moments on the bidding order then I moved on. The terror had escalated and seized me. I couldn't draw a breath.

I saw Ron from a distance. He was flitting around the

auction site talking to various people, none of whom I recognized. I couldn't handle talking to him right now, as my pulse was unsteady. There would be plenty of time later.

Mark was nowhere in sight, but that did not surprise me. He seemed too light in spirit the last few days and showed no interest in our progress or the auction. I considered it a blessing that he did not show. We didn't need his bad energy permeating our hope.

I left the auction site and went to the underground parking garage to rest in my car and inhale fresh oxygen from the portable tank I now kept close. I sat in the drivers seat with my head leaning back on the headrest, but my knuckles were so tightly gripping the steering wheel that my hands began to burn.

I stayed in my car trying to calm down. Twenty minutes before the auction, I climbed the stairs praying that a huge crowd would be present. My worst nightmare met me instead.

There were only eighteen people seated in an area intended for over three hundred. Of the eighteen attending, only three registered to bid. As the bidding began and the minimum bids were ignored, my heart began to palpitate wildly. The auction was a dismal failure. Thirty-eight properties were offered and only one woman bid.

I refused to look at anyone but rather stared right through the podium. Long after the auction ended I was still sitting, my spirit completely deflated. I stumbled to my car and drove home in a stupor.

•   •   •

It was painfully obvious that we were out of business. The investors would lose everything and I could not imagine how I would ever be free of Mark. He would finally get his wish in bankruptcy court as our company would not survive and the creditors would circle quickly. All the massive staff effort, beautifully constructed brochures, ads in all the publications, promises from real estate offices for attendance and still, the turnout was dismal.

Years later, I was told by an agent that Mark had made dozens of calls notifying every real estate office that the auction had been cancelled. No agent thought to question his claims.

•   •   •

I have no memory of the remainder of the weekend, that dangerous vortex I had feared for so long had finally swallowed me.

Chapter 58

Monday morning I went to the office very early and quietly waited for the staff to arrive. I made a tour of the entire office, reminiscing over moments that had ended in unabridged laughter. They were few.

When I reached Mark's office I took a deep breath, turned the doorknob and entered the room. His office was full of shadows, cold and clammy. My skin began to prickle. The air was heavy with hostility and deranged behavior. The hatred began to ring in my ears as a cascade of memories flooded the room.

"What the hell is wrong with you? I'm sick of looking at your haggard face…"

"You idiot! How could you be so stupid?"

"Monica is useless. Why the hell did you bring her to our company?"

"I can't believe I married you. I'm embarrassed…"

I could see his twisted façade as he spit out each insult. My skin stood on edge as if I was in imminent danger. Instinctively I slammed the door shut. I regretted unveiling the memories that room held.

I made the journey back to my office and sat at my desk staring aimlessly. How many hours had I spent in this room over the past two years? With all the horrible memories, it still looked beautiful to me. The moment I had refused to acknowledge was now confronting me.

I had to let the staff go and close up the company. All the investors had to be notified and contractor's bids cancelled. I had to shut it all down and put the whole debacle into a distant memory in a safe segment of my mind.

Not only would the investors lose their investments but I was certainly bankrupt. There was no way to recover from this large a loss. Mark is the only one that seemed unaffected by the turnout.

I saw him briefly on Sunday. His attitude was smug and he did not ask any questions. I assumed he had already spoken to Ron. He showered quickly and left. He hadn't been back since. I didn't care but only wondered how our marriage would end. It was inevitable, but my immediate concern was closing the company. I would deal with my sham of a marriage later.

•   •   •

The staff began to arrive and went into the conference room. Monica did not show. The walls were quiet as no words were necessary. Ron's team did not materialize, which was a welcomed relief. We had not spoken since the auction. I'd deal with him later.

Tina checked the voicemail while we waited for the remainder of the staff. She came into the conference room with a look of horror.

"What is it Tina?" My breath was tight.

"Monica… that was her mother. She is in the hospital.

She had a breakdown." Tina was barely talking.

"Oh my god." Was all I could say.

What was happening to all of us? I had a terrible sense of guilt, as I knew the stress of the company was the contributing factor. I saw it happening and yet did not reach for her. What was wrong with me!

Monica had been losing weight and was becoming progressively short-tempered. Unfortunately, I was so involved in my own nightmare that I didn't attempt to lend her aid, as I should have. We were each caught in our own hell, with no one to protect us.

Monica came to this company because of me. She suffered an inordinate threshold of abuse from Mark. He hated her loyalty to me and resented her unwillingness to abandon me over the years. Now Monica was lost and I had helped push her over the edge. My guilt was profound, as I knew I had culpability in her demise.

The conference room held a deeper level of silence then I ever thought possible. My final comments to the staff remain a blur. They filtered out of the room with tears in their eyes. I knew most of what they shed was for Monica.

Chapter 59

We had no time to grieve as the office had to be torn down immediately. The files, furniture, computers, telephone system and a multitude of details were pressing.

Tina and Lora took the lead and boxed, labeled and dismantled the office in record time.

Everything would go to a storage unit until I had time to sort and sell. We had five days. The movers would arrive on Saturday, and I still had Ron and the investors to deal with. Mark had moved on to bankruptcy mode. He was energized.

Mark met with an attorney and began assembling all the relevant documents. He strolled through the filing room collecting real estate files with a spring in his step. He never expressed regret or demonstrated any act of remorse. He had the innate ability to not feel guilt. It was truly as if he was born into this world without a conscience.

He couldn't have been more separate from me. I felt culpable for every loss. My guilt ate at me and began to devour my essence. I watched my world being dismantled and wondered what would become of me. Could I survive? Where would I go? What would happen to the investors? Would any of us prevail over our connection to Mark? I questioned how anyone could.

·   ·   ·

I tried to telephone Monica a few times throughout the week. She wasn't taking calls. Her mother was cold and would not accept any words of encouragement. I eventually drove to her home and my knocks echoed off the closed door. I knew they all blamed me. I held myself responsible.

Chapter 60

On Tuesday morning amidst the packing, Ron and I finally met in my office. He came in tight and controlled, but clearly shaken.

"What happens from here?" Ron inquired.

"Well, I've thought about it. I can sign ownership of the properties over to you. At least you will be able to collect whatever monies are possible. Everything else will be decided in bankruptcy court, but there's nothing to fight over." I was waiting for the explosion. It didn't come.

"I'll have the Quit Claim Deeds and paperwork drawn today. I want to decide how each is sold." It was a demand.

"Fine. Are you going to contact all the investors? Somehow I don't think Mark will, and many I've never spoken to." I asked softly.

"Yeah, I'll handle it. When are you moving?" He asked sharply.

"Saturday morning. Everything will go in a storage unit. Listen Ron, I'm sorry. I just can't do it anymore. I'm very sick and we can't keep shuffling the losses around. We just keep digging the hole deeper."

"You should have stayed in just to help me recover my money. I don't care how sick you are, you owe me!" He spit it at me.

"I can't Ron. I just can't do this anymore. It's killing me. And Mark, well, you know we can't depend on him."

I was so hoping he would just try to see my point of view. Instead, his eyes narrowed and became hard.

"I'm sorry I ever met you two." He hurled the comment at me and left the room.

I knew he would never forgive me as he lost just under two million dollars.

•   •   •

The office was packed up and ready to close Friday afternoon. I scarcely remember the disassembly of the company. My well had dried up long ago, making it physically and emotionally impossible to contribute to the dismantling.

I was even too tired to cry. Mark was busy with our personal and corporate bankruptcy and rarely came home. When he did, it was only to collect my signature on the court documents.

He would pace the floor while I tried to understand the legalese. All I could see where pages of creditors and numbers constituting the few years we spent together.

I saw my assets float across the page, mixed with hundreds of Trust Deeds and an inventory of office expenses and construction invoices. My life's work was relegated to a few columns on a list of expenditures.

My health limited any involvement in either. I had no idea whether I could keep my house or my car. It didn't really matter - I couldn't afford either.

Chapter 61

*A*fter the company closed my body absolutely shut down. It was as if every ounce of energy I had only brought me through the closure. Once that was completed, my health crumbled. My energy drained out of me, like a water hose that went dry. My sense of defeat reigned supreme and I gave into my condition.

When I met Mark in 1991, my world was prosperous with material success, physical health, friends and accomplishment. Here it was, mid-1995 and I had lost it all. My world couldn't have been any emptier if I was homeless.

I knew my marriage was over as the façade melted long ago. Once the legal proceedings were finished we would go our separate ways. Each area of my life was being redefined. I had lost my marriage, money, security, health and most of my family and friends. Even my relationship with MJ was all but gone.

It was as if a fierce storm had ripped through my world and stripped each element away. It was hard to think back over the years and see how each facet was taken. I felt robbed but could not identify the thief. My world was flattened and what remained were tiny fragmented pieces. It was akin to a glass bowl being dropped from a mile high and shattering into a million slivers of glass. Could it really be reconstructed, and if so, what would it look like?

All I wanted was to start over. I didn't want to explore where it all went wrong, or how Mark changed, or why the business collapsed. It was all a mistake that I needed to run from. I wanted to put as much distance from the whole lurid situation as possible. Unfortunately there was not an ounce of energy remaining to rebuild my life. And what was worse, I had no idea where to start.

Chapter 62

Tina and I met early Saturday morning outside our building to wait for the movers. I didn't want to go back inside as it was difficult to see my life stuffed into boxes.

Mark claimed he was spending the day with the bankruptcy attorney but I suspected he was with his new conquest. He was taking extra care with his appearance and I remembered all too well how he used to do that for me. It should have hurt but I was numb to his duplicity.

The company accounts were closed on Friday and the utilities were turned off. The skeletal remains were all that lingered. We sat in awkward silence. It had all been said. The movers arrived and we all walked inside. I unlocked the front door and pushed it open.

Tina stepped in first and said, "What the hell?"

I slid past her. "What . . . happened to everything?" I was shocked.

The office was empty. I picked up my pace and examined every room. It was all gone. The desks, computers, artwork, files everything. The office was empty. Finally I wandered into my office space and saw a small pile of remnants from my desk. Tampons, Kleenex and a few other personal items were strewn across the floor. I knew exactly what happened.

"Damn it! Ron!"

I flew out the building to my car to use my phone. I punched in Ron's number and sent it ripping across the circuits. He didn't answer. It rolled to his voicemail.

"This is Alesandra. You have thirty minutes to get back over here or I'm calling the cops!" I barely held my fury.

I marched back up to the office and asked the movers to get a cup of coffee at the deli around the corner. I told them it would be thirty minutes or so. I tried to contain my rage until Ron arrived. I was certain he would.

In twenty minutes he pushed his way in the front door, a look of steely amusement across his face.

"You owe me money, so I took what was left." He said it with pride.

"Where is it?" My eyes were hard little dots.

"Safe." His resolve lifted just a tiny fraction.

"I mean it, where is it?" I repeated.

"In my office. I'm not giving it back." He sounded petulant.

"You can have most of it, but not the files. They are corporate property." I was threatening and Ron knew it.

"You owe me a hell of a lot more than the furniture." He said as he turned to walk down the hallway.

Ron housed his real estate company on the same floor as our company. I followed him past his office suite to yet another door at the end of the hall. He took out a key and opened the office. All of my furnishings were sitting like prizes. He looked defiant.

I glanced around to see what I really needed. Most of

it could be sacrificed. It would save me the cost of storing it. Then I laid eyes on my desk. It was the desk my father bought me and I funneled all my rage. I stormed over to the cherry structure and planted my body on it.

"I'm not leaving without my desk and files."

It was years of frustration that powered into one moment. This was the only tiny fraction of control I had and I wouldn't budge.

"No. You can have the files. That's it." Ron seemed amused.

"I'm not leaving unless I get my desk. I'll call the cops and file a burglary complaint. I mean it! I want my desk."

I had a focal point for my anger and must have looked ridiculous. I was a skinny woman who could barely stand up, in bankruptcy, fighting for a desk. But I was feeling crazy and Ron saw it. The desk was the only thing left I could fight for.

"Fine, take the stupid desk. Get out." He acquiesced and I seized the moment.

I told Tina to get the movers and collect the file cabinets and my desk. It was loaded in twenty minutes and moved to my home as the storage unit would no longer be necessary. I left the building forever.

Chapter 63

After the company closed and the bankruptcy was filed, Mark and I received an instantaneous response from the investors and creditors. Everyone was jockeying for position to ensure their position was secure in court. The cessation of the company was fast, but the bankruptcy proceedings were painfully slow.

I tried not to think of what would become of me after the court discharged the debt. I would lose the house - that was certain. Where would I move? I knew it wouldn't be with Mark, but I had no idea how I would come up with the money for a small rental. Even if I had the deposit, how would I pay the monthly bills?

I had used any reservoir of strength to close the company and therefore let Mark handle the bankruptcy. What difference did it make how the papers were filed? The underlying truth was that we lost everything. No amount of negotiating could change that fact. I acquiesced easily.

Mark's lack of remorse let him navigate the bankruptcy with ease. He never showed signs of strain, but rather it was the opposite. He seemed free and light in a way I could never imagine being again. His broad smile and laugh began to cut me as if they were edges of a sharp knife dissecting my soul.

If I could have moved I would have. But I felt truly lost. I wanted to hide and heal. Neither would be possible but I pretended this was not my sealed fate but rather a time to reassess. I did neither. My world was black and how I spent my days is still a mystery. I did not leave the house, nor did I read, or watch TV. The memory is wiped from my existence. I suspect they were too painful and I have eliminated them.

I was sure whatever acts Mark took in the company would be lost forever, buried in the mound of debt that constituted our brief marriage. My debts were simple in comparison to the overwhelming volume of corporate loss. Each property had multiple Trust Deeds, contractor bills, agent's fees and outstanding taxes. It was a sizable debt I'm sure that was rarely seen in the courts.

Although I had signed the properties over to Ron, the lenders and investors sent notifications of foreclosure for the multitude of properties we owned both personally and corporately. They were trying to protect themselves in the proceedings.

Process servers attacked the house on regular intervals. I didn't answer the door but the constant stress was overwhelming.

Mark managed to stay out until late into the night most of the time, leaving me alone to defend against the assaults. My nerves were frayed and my resolve weakened.

Chapter 64

*T*he next few weeks were a mixture of increased head-aches, diarrhea and horrid stomachaches. The seizures began to diminish with the change in medication, but the Depakote made me blow up. The scales climbed 30 lbs and continued to increase. Within three months I had gained over 65 pounds with the scales tipping over 180 lbs. I knew the explosion of weight after being emaciated could not be healthy but I was willing to stay on the meds to control the seizures.

I was told to keep a constant seizure journal to docu-ment the progress of treatment. My life was relegated to keep-ing notes of my bowel habits, seizure activities and other symptoms. It was a horrid existence as my body continued to expand.

My world shrunk and my lightness of being diminished. I would glance at myself in the mirror as seldom as possible, convinced I was gaining weight by the hour.

What was worse was that I didn't care. I missed my world in its entirety but as the symptoms increased, my connec-tion to living grew thin. Each day was a struggle and I couldn't imagine what was happening to me.

My sinuses felt compacted and it was hard to breathe through my nose. Headaches were constant and piercing with tremendous light sensitivity. All water tasted metallic and my throat felt full, as if I was growing masses that made it all but impossible to swallow. My hair was brittle and thin and bore no resemblance to the thick head of hair I was once proud of. But it mattered little, as I no longer socialized.

My world was crumbling and all I cared about was the ability to make it through a day without a seizure.

Chapter 65

My marriage to Mark would be linked until the legal proceedings were over. He took another job and was our only source of income, as meager as it was. Although our marriage was finished, I was unsure how to extricate myself, as I couldn't work. We held onto this fraudulent portrait of a marriage out of necessity.

Conversation was stilted in clouds of tension. But I knew deep inside that he was preparing to leave. He had ripped through my life with the ferocity and devastation of a hurricane, and soon he would leave to find another game.

Why he stayed through the bankruptcy troubled me. But I came to realize that he needed my signature on documents and wanted to make sure the discharge was finished before he moved on to his next woman. I was used up.

The home that once represented my imminent hope became my prison. I left for doctor's appointments and to fill prescriptions. Other than those meager outings my world was silent.

Chapter 66

I wanted to reach for MJ but Mark threatened to move instantly and cut off the power to the house. He blamed her for the distance between us and would only agree to provide the basic necessities if I did not communicate with her. I didn't dare take the chance, as my situation was grave.

Although our home was held solely in my name, without Mark's willingness to provide financial support I would be without the means to survive.

I didn't know if MJ would even talk to me again, and I couldn't risk reaching for her and then losing the small amount of support Mark provided. I remained silent and let my world shrink further.

The day was coming soon where I would have to find an alternate means to endure, but I was at a loss as to how that would happen.

I was still waiting for notification from the State of California on my disability claim. Dr. Bakst had filed the paperwork and my case was under review. I just prayed the disability would come through before the discharge date.

I shuffled around the house and lightly cleaned, as we could no longer afford the luxury of household help. I divided laundry for hours and washed Mark's separate from mine. I didn't even want our clothes touching. I stared at a large load of Mark's whites tumbling around the washer and a voice within reared up. I grabbed a red tee shirt and threw it in the mix. It turned the load pink. I smiled and left it.

Mark began leaving me for days at a time. When he did come home he would shower, grab a change of clothes, get my signature on a few papers for the court and leave again.

After the way he charged at me a few months earlier, I was afraid to challenge him. My back was never the same yet I could not imagine seeing yet another doctor. I could tolerate the pain, what I couldn't take was another altercation with him. I knew he was busy setting up where he would land next and I was sure it involved a woman.

I wondered if I would ever want another relationship. All I wanted was my freedom.

As the creditors meeting drew near, his temper could not be contained. He began staying at the house nearly every night and the early morning calls from our attorney only fueled his anger. Testimony had to be reviewed and the numbers studied to handle any questions during the appearance. It was the first time in months that Mark appeared to be nervous.

Chapter 67

In January of 1996, the day of the creditors meeting arrived. It is a forum where creditors may probe the debtor's estate to determine the legitimacy of the bankruptcy petition. The court appointed a trustee to oversee the evaluation of the estate and regulate any transfer of property through the proceedings.

California bankruptcy code required that a creditors meeting be convened within thirty days after the order for relief was entered with the court. Any creditor was entitled to be present and ask questions regarding the estate. I knew it would be a full house.

Mark asked me to stay home the day of court. He suggested the stress would be overwhelming. I agreed, grateful for his protection even though I knew it was self-serving. He wanted total control. I was delighted to give it to him.

Late in the day the house was besieged again, only this time it was MJ. I had a terrible day and was lying in my bedroom, somewhere between the worlds. My head hurt and my heart was skipping beats. The house exploded with the sound of the doorbell. MJ was drumming the bell, filling the house with the horrifying sound. I buried my head deeper trying to block out the racket. Eventually the noise stopped. A few moments later I heard the windows rattling and MJ's muffled angry voice.

"Alesandra, open the damn door!" She screamed.

I ignored her and dug deeper into my covers.

"…He's setting you up." She was screaming.

I didn't know what she was yelling about. What now? Why couldn't MJ just let me heal? Mark was due home any second and I didn't want her to be inside. It would cause even more turmoil. I took my pillow and jammed it against my ears. Eventually the sound faded. The windows stopped rattling. I dozed.

I will always regret not answering the door.

Chapter 68

*A*nyone that has endured a serious illness or major surgery can attest to the inconsistency of time. It passes without merit. Hours are lost in a fugue of pain or misguided sleep. The second hand travels slowly, as if the clock is mocking a life once lived. It is a horrid passage of sunrise to sunset, through the blackest of nights.

Days are marked by the tiniest of accomplishments. The relevant size of your framework shrivels. Mine went from traveling the world, to the entire city of San Diego, then dwindled to the suite of business offices, then to my home – finally to my room.

I suffered day after day in painful silence. My only guide was the hunger of Selsie and Zeff. Their beseeching cries would push me from my bed. I would hug the walls, moving in tiny steps, attempting to cover the distance from the master bedroom to the kitchen, to ease their deprivation. They were fed whatever was close-at-hand. I know they were neglected – that pains me still. Yet Selsie remained dutiful. She knew her mom was in trouble. She watched me for hours, days. No one visited. The phone became silent. I could not reach out.

How did I survive? Who brought groceries? How did the days pass? I may never know the answers. All I have is a black memory of seizures, pain and depression.

Mark was still my husband of record although he rarely stayed at the house. He may have paid the bills and supplied the elementary requirements of the household. Whatever his involvement, it left no lasting memory. I suspect his cruelty continued and therefore I disconnected the thread in my mind.

Chapter 69

I don't know when MJ stopped reaching out. All I knew was that she was gone. I had pushed her from my life. Why hadn't I listened? She had no ulterior motive. Yet I could not call her. She would have answered. It was my decision - one that extended my torment much longer than was necessary. It must have been maddening for her to watch me descend into hell with the devil. For her own sanity, she had to pull away and wait – pray that I could find the courage to rise again and leave Mark.

I tried to talk to my mom, but I was so embarrassed over my demise that I cut my calls short. I rarely called her and when I did, I would wrap the call in a matter of moments. My friends all dwindled away. Some called a few times and didn't know what to say. Others never tried.

I never understood the psychological torment of battered women. I suppose part of me thought them weak and unwilling to stand up for themselves. Why didn't they just say *enough*? But the mental isolation that transpires in an abusive relationship is nothing short of psychological propaganda. It happens slowly, over many hours, days, in arguments and love-making or in discrete phrases or looks. I never saw it happening, it just was.

To understand a battered woman blueprint, one must first understand how someone becomes "battered." I believe the cycle of battering consists of three distinct phases. First is the pressure phase, followed by the explosion, culminating in a calm, loving respite.

Talk to anyone in a horrid relationship. They live for the last phase. The moment he is subdued, remorseful, even kind. It seems as if it could never happen again. That is exactly how one is trapped – from one episode to the next. Shocked each time it occurs, initially appeased that his moment of awareness creates a calm atmosphere. Eventually appalled that you are trapped in a situation – and you have no idea how to extract yourself.

Abuse occurs on many levels. The most obvious is physical – the bruises, broken bones, all bodily signs. Another insidious, less visible brutality is psychological. The constant games and ruses are tiresome, exhausting, more than I could bear. Eventually my strength evaded me. I felt like a victim. One of the weak women I did not understand.

Mark was a master at psychological games. He had a way of making every irrational thought seem sane. I became convinced of the unfathomable. My family was trying to break up our marriage. The investors were greedy. MJ was jealous and didn't really love me. My friends did not care. My psychologist only wanted money. No one truly cared about me. I was alone – except for him.

He knew exactly how to play the subtle chords of doubt. He knew how to extract the tiniest beads of strength from my argument. As my illness deepened, so did his hold over me. I grew tired of arguing. It was less exhausting to just listen. I would doze to his litany and awaken to yet another reason why I shouldn't communicate with my friends, twin or business associates.

Eventually my isolation became absolute. I have no doubt Mark was pushing me toward the cliff of suicide. He knew my history and he knew my fear. Yet, in spite of his mastery of psychological warfare, one connection he did not understand was my love for the cats. Had he known, they would have been sacrificed. Of that I am certain.

Chapter 70

One day the cord snapped and I did leave. It happened quickly and without question. It was shortly after the creditors meeting, while we were waiting for verification that the bankruptcy discharge was filed. It was March of 1996, just a few weeks from what would have been our three-year anniversary. I don't know what precipitated his attack, but he had the look of hate in his eyes and I was in his path.

Mark came home in a foul mood. He looked as if he wanted to smash something. I recognized the look from the office, just before he would punch a hole in the wall.

I was in the family room lying on the couch with an icepack on my back. He strode in and threw a file on the coffee table and held his stride on the way to the kitchen.

"Sign the papers." He barked the order.

"What papers? I thought we were done." I started to sit up to reach for the file, but my back spasm brought me back down.

"Just sign the damn things. I've only got a few minutes." His face was dark and his eyes were black rather than blue.

I rolled onto my side and reached for the paperwork. I began to take them out of the folder to review. Mark rushed in from the kitchen and snarled at me.

"Just sign them!" He snatched the folder out of my hands and pulled it open to the signature page. He threw the paper at me and pulled a pen out of his pocket and flung it on the table.

I was sitting upright and reached for the front page of the document.

"No, I'm going to look them over."

I didn't see him lunge for me and certainly couldn't have moved quickly enough even if I had. The next thing I knew I was on the floor. My neck hurt and it took a minute to get my bearings and realize that he had backhanded me.

I wrestled my body away from the furniture and scooted out of striking distance.

I grabbed the papers and without knowing what it was, I signed his name, a dangerous move with him standing over me. My crafty effort paid off. He never looked at the paper and just grabbed it and left. He went to the guest room for a long time then left through the garage door.

My heart was slamming in my chest cavity. I was still sitting on the floor with the pain in my back excruciating. This time I was convinced that whatever he dislodged the first time had broken free, as I heard a large pop when I hit the ground. I waited for him to leave and called the police. An emergency restraining order was filed and I changed the locks.

I had divorce papers filed immediately.

Chapter 71

After he left the days past slowly -- without memory or accomplishment. Each morning I would slip from the safety of the dream world only to realize time and again the nightmare was not limited to my dreamtime. It was inescapable regardless of my conscious state. Some days I would wake to the remnants of my bodily functions during a seizure. I would use every ounce of energy to change the linens, shower and return to a horizontal state.

My back eventually healed and the bruises dissipated, but internally I never forgot his blows. The seizures returned and consumed my existence.

On rare occasions I could sit in another room for a few hours, oblivious of the outer world, and unaware of how to improve my lot within the walls of my prison. The only time I left my house was to keep the myriad of doctor's appointments. Medications were increased and my life slowed to a snails pace, documented only by the log of seizures I was required to keep.

I have never experienced time as constant, yet its curse was most deeply felt in poor health. The clock was painfully slow -- some moments surely felt as if they would never pass. I still lived in a gorgeous home -- for how long was unclear. Yet it no longer held any meaning.

The eucalyptus canyons could just have easily been a junkyard. There was no pull from nature. My legs could not carry me past the back door. My vision was blurred and my spirit flat. My stomach ached and my skin was wet from perspiration, yet my body always felt cold and clammy.

Selsie and Zeff provided my only sense of comfort. I never closed the bedroom door anymore, as the heat generated from their little bodies warmed more than my outer skin. Their purring and constant vigil became a welcome sense that something outside my horror was still important.

Selsie, my loyal little lady, was deeply concerned and rarely left my side. Often I would wake to her little body tucked close to my heart. Her head was generally buried deep within my pillow -- her breath mixing with mine. Her scent eased my pounding head, and her comfort provided a thread to life. She never begged for food and as the days passed she lost more weight. But her constant presence is the only thing that kept me on this planet.

Zeff on the other hand was still consumed with wanderlust spirit, and would often beg that the outer skin of the house be split. There were many mornings I did not remember opening either the patio or the side door of the master bedroom. I did not monitor their movement, as life had no meaning. I loved these little creatures, but the continuous seizures and horrible side effects from the drugs made my motherly instincts dull. I had no desire to live. I had nothing to offer the world.

Then the foreclosure notice arrived. I only had about four months before I would be physically removed from my home.

Chapter 72

Somehow I found the strength to put an ad in the newspaper to sell off my furniture, anything to stretch my time in the house. I even sold the stove and dishwasher as I never cooked and didn't need the appliances. The cash was used to bring the house payments current and it bought me another six months. I prayed it would be enough. I was terrified to move and even more frightened to stay. It was clearly more than I could afford, but I just didn't know how to begin the process of moving. I was paralyzed and clung to the only refuge I knew - my home.

In late September 1996, Mark's attorney eventually contacted me to arrange a time for Mark to pick up his belongings. As the restraining order was in affect, Mark could not contact me directly. We arranged for early evening and after we hung up, I called the police to have them keep the peace. Having the police present was the only way to keep the force of the restraining order in place.

They arrived about 15 minutes before Mark and reviewed the restraining order. Mark arrived promptly at 7:00

p.m. and was livid when I opened the door and he saw two cops behind me. It was only a matter of moments before he was in full tempo, screaming loudly for them to leave. Eventually one officer tried to calm Mark and it led to a tussle that ended with Mark on the kitchen floor - handcuffed to instill control. He was given two choices – leave or be arrested. He opted to leave and in his anger, never took any of his belongings.

The following day Mark's attorney called again to arrange another meeting. I refused and stated that I would not go through the embarrassment a second time. I declared that his belongings were going to Goodwill, and any remaining items would be discarded.

Chapter 73

$\mathcal{T}$he remainder of 1996, I was able to stay in my home. I eventually had to sell off my collection of art to keep the creditors satisfied. This bought me another four months or so. I watched my prize possessions leave the front door for a fraction of what they were worth, without any sense of loss. I was too sick to care and I needed more time before moving.

As the day drew closer, my spirits were even more deflated. My approval for State of California disability finally came through but only provided minimal relief – nothing that would pay rent. It would be many months before I knew anything regarding Federal Disability.

I needed to move – but where? I couldn't afford San Diego any longer, and I longed to leave the pain behind.

Chapter 74

My depression deepened, as I could no longer remember what it felt like to have a life. The darkness filled my existence and with it came the pervasive sense that I would never recover. But each time the thought of hopelessness slid into my mind, a tiny voice always guided me back to the possibility that my life could come full circle.

I had no idea how to shake the guilt that filled my mind every time I thought of the company failing. I didn't know what happened to the investors, or if they were able to recover any money after the bankruptcy. If any ended up as I did, it was bleak.

I never heard anything about Mark, as I no longer engaged the world. My existence centered on trying to improve my health.

Just as I thought it couldn't get any worse, I awoke one morning with the most excruciating pain in my right leg. I was convinced I tore my hamstring as it felt as if a hot torch was burning through my muscle. I could not walk. I took a taxi to the hospital, where I was given morphine to alleviate the pain.

The ER physician reassured me that my hamstring was

not damaged, but he could not pinpoint the cause of the pain. I was devastated - another unknown failure in my body. The next week was spent in an orthopedic surgeon's office with a diagnosis of Reflex Sympathetic Dystrophy, an overactive response of the nervous system that causes severe pain. The cause was unknown. The cure involved a series of injections into my spinal column. It was agonizing and did nothing to alleviate the pain. I felt hopeless.

I was taking handfuls of pills every day. The numbers were staggering at well over two thousand per month. The colorful piles in my hands looked like pieces of candy, but couldn't have felt further from the tasty sweets.

Dr. Braun had me on a cocktail of medications and I was on a new anti-seizure drug from Dr. Bakst that I was told would not have the dreaded side effect of weight gain. The orthopedic added strong painkillers to the mix, including Oxycontin and Dilaudid. I was slamming down pills and in constant pain, with my despair deepening daily. This was no way to live.

Chapter 75

Melissa, my psychologist was fighting to keep me on this planet, and we knew that if I lost more ground the chances were slim. My immune system had absolutely no ability to fight infection, leaving me riddled with medical complications. My lungs were in terrible condition, as I had reoccurring pneumonia more times than I could count.

I had been seeing Melissa for several years, and she was the one person that refused to let me pull away during the horror. She never charged me to work with her, as she knew the precarious financial position I was in. Melissa just cared deeply and I clung to her.

She often questioned the excessive amounts of medications prescribed by the psychiatrist, but couldn't question his medical advice. Finally, she suggested that I move to her hometown of Santa Fe, New Mexico and spend time recovering my health. She still had many connections there and offered to help me find a place to live.

I grasped her offer, as New Mexico was much more affordable, and I desperately wanted to leave San Diego – it held nothing but pain for me.

Chapter 76

Since I had sold everything possible to exist, and therefore had only a few pieces of furniture and the less valuable art, there was not much to pack.

There were boxes of office files in the garage, as well as a few that had Mark's handwriting on them. I did not recognize them, and must have overlooked them when I gave his clothes to Goodwill. I was too overwhelmed to deal with them, as anything regarding business would only remind me of what I lost. I would face them someday, when I was well.

I decided to store the boxes at a friend's garage instead. I would move to Santa Fe with very little and find a way to begin picking up the pieces.

Melissa arranged for a moving company who offered to bring my items to Santa Fe free of charge, as he had a load of furniture going east. Her kindness was overwhelming.

•   •   •

Zeff had mysteriously disappeared a few weeks before

the move. It was down to Selsie and myself. I barely grieved Zeff's loss and felt I could not take any more suffering.

I had an overpowering sense of relief as I flew out of San Diego. I hoped never to set eyes on the city again.

Melissa had located a sweet, one room studio in Santa Fe. It was cheap and situated next to a heroin house, something I was certain she didn't know, but it mattered little, as I was grateful for her help. Clearly I was not going to live in an afflu-ent area during this phase of my life.

I was just relieved to have a small place that I could call my own. I telephoned my mother and told her my plans. I asked her to keep my new telephone number private. She was the only person who knew where I was as I looked at this phase in my life as a chance to heal.

Chapter 77

During the move, I misplaced my prescription for pain meds and between the sitting and unpacking, my pain skyrocketed. I telephoned my doctor in San Diego and explained the situation. I was informed that the prescription would not be replaced, as it was a three-part controlled substance. I was being taught a lesson.

They agreed to furnish a lesser painkiller instead, but when I went to the pharmacy, I was told the risk of stopping the powerful painkillers cold turkey – it was too dangerous. The pharmacist recommended I go to the emergency room. This turned out to be a blessing that began my healing process.

•   •   •

A wonderful general practitioner named Dr. Ashton was covering the ER, and immediately sensed the legitimacy of my pain. By the time I arrived at the hospital, I was out of medication and the pain was unbearable. I was crying in deep sobs and felt I couldn't take the excruciating throbbing. She checked my vital signs, then sat down across from me.

Dr. Ashton went on to explain that she believed my pain was very real, but that she doubted it was Reflex Sympathetic Dystrophy as was originally diagnosed. There was some testing she wanted to do first.

I still had a cobra policy for health insurance, and was encouraged for the first time in many months. Dr. Ashton stated an MRI was needed, and that someone would call me with the testing date. Then she proceeded to prescribe the painkillers.

We scheduled the MRI and waited for the results.

Chapter 78

A week later Dr. Ashton's office telephoned, asking me to come in to discuss the results. What it revealed both excited and terrified me. I had blown my lower spine in several regions – L3 down through L4 and the most severe was at the lowest part of the L5/S1 – a massive herniation that was impinging the nerve root down my leg. This also explained the extreme bladder pressure I had been experiencing for months.

I thought back to the physical blows I received from Mark, and remembered the loud pop in my back. Now it all made sense. I told no one out of shame.

My injury was complicated by an advanced case of spinal stenosis, a narrowing of the spinal canal. The narrowing was aggravating the herniations, as the protruding discs were pinching the nerves in the spinal cord. It required surgery as quickly as possible.

Dr. Ashton apologized for the medical community's gross error, and reassured me the pain would be alleviated after surgery. I hugged her and expressed deep gratitude. I was scheduled for the surgery, and she assured me that the neurosurgeon that would be performing the surgery was one of their best. I left her office hopeful.

While I was waiting for my surgery date, I decided to see an acupuncturist to help control the severe pain.

Barbara was an earthy woman, tall and lean. Her face looked scrubbed fresh, and she glowed like a woman in a Dove commercial.

She was the first healthcare provider that actually showed an interest in discovering the root of the mysterious seizures. She believed a toxic substance was to blame, but she wanted to do a hair analysis to verify her suspicion. The test sample went off and I was told it would take 4-6 weeks to get the results.

Chapter 79

I underwent spinal surgery in July of 1997 – fourteen weeks after moving. The day of my procedure my nerves were frayed. I feared paralysis and had excessive panic rising. But through it all, a hope rose that my agony would be alleviated and help me begin the road back to health.

A neighbor agreed to care for Selsie during the week I was in the hospital. She was a lovely retired woman who loved animals as I did. I knew Selsie would be in good hands.

I awoke in post-op and my first sensation was the absence of pain. Even after the magnitude of the operation, the intense nerve pain was gone. I could not have been more relieved. I was sent home a week later with a follow-up appointment in ten days.

I took a taxi home and laid quiet for the next ten days. The surgery left me weak and I couldn't drive to get groceries. I lived on boxed mashed potatoes, as that was all that was in my cupboard.

Ten days later and 15 lbs lighter I returned for my follow-up appointment. The surgeon was mortified that I lost so much weight, and after I explained that I was new in town and just couldn't get out to grocery shop, he grunted and left the examining room. He returned with the card of an organization called *Kitchen Angels*, a group that supplied hot meals to AIDS patients in town. He had placed a call and asked them to add me to their delivery, along with food for Selsie.

I was at a loss for words – his compassion was heartfelt and touched a place within me that I didn't know survived. The kind act of yet another human soul was almost too much to describe.

Over the next few weeks, the sweetest retired women delivered hot meals everyday. They brought food for Selsie and as I recovered, I felt the contact from other kind women.

My life was simple and had promise.

Chapter 80

$\mathcal{B}$arbara finally called and told me that the test results of my hair analysis were in. She would not give them to me by phone, and insisted we wait until I was strong enough to come by her office. It was another six weeks before we sat down to discuss the hair analysis.

I was handed the results and saw outrageously high levels of both Mercury and Boron – much more than I could have received through mercury fillings. Her question is what made me go cold.

"Alesandra, is there any way you could have been exposed to poison?" Barbara stated it simply and without emotion.

I felt the color drain from my entire body. MJ's words rang in my head. I felt a pang of shame for the way I treated her.

"I don't know, I guess it's possible," I muttered.

"What do you mean, possible?" She cocked her head in curiosity.

"Well, my sister always suspected my ex-husband was poisoning me. I thought... well... I didn't believe her." Disgrace was coloring my skin a bright red.

"Well, it appears someone was feeding you high doses of mercury and boron. The levels are too high to be caused by even a mouth full of metal." It was clear Barbara wanted to ask a million questions, but she didn't push. Her forehead held some incredulous wrinkles.

"Is there a way to get it out of my body?" I said it so softly that I wasn't sure she heard me.

"Definitely."

She began to outline a type of natural therapy but I only heard snippets as I was still in shock. I accepted a series of appointments and left with my thoughts racing wildly.

Chapter 81

I floated home in a haze, and began to research Mercury and its effect on the body. The symptoms rang out like my diary – insomnia, poor memory, irritability, depression, weight loss and exhaustion. Even the hair loss was part of the equation. It brought tears to my eyes.

My little apartment squeezed me and I left to roam the plaza, staring blankly at the Pueblo women selling jewelry. I felt separate from the world, as the reality of the venom began to settle.

I wandered into the Cathedral and felt the peace permeate the pews. I sat and gazed at nothing – my vision went inward.

The contradictions of the past six years were crashing wildly. An image of Mark bringing me coffee crept into my mind.

MJ's words bit in, "*I think he's trying to kill you.*"
His wounded voice, "*Aren't you going to drink it?*"
"*You've got to listen to me!*" MJ pleaded.
"*Please don't worry, I'd never do anything to hurt you.*"
"*You were healthy when you met him!*"

"I want to be your best friend. MJ's always been jealous of you."

How could I have not seen it?

I felt dirty. I headed home and stripped off my clothes to wash off the horrid realizations. I scrubbed my body and washed my hair until I was sure that any exterior remnant was removed.

I stepped out of the shower and wrapped towels around my body and over my wet hair. I wiped the fog off the mirror and stared at my reflection.

It was through the haze of steam that I took the towel off my head and stared at my hair. It hung in large wet ringlets nearly to the middle of my back. I touched it lightly and retracted my hand, convinced the poison was oozing from the hair shafts. I knew what I had to do.

I stumbled into the other room and took a pair of scissors from the drawer. Armed with my savior I returned to the bathroom. I held sections of hair away from my head and brought the blades up. The first cut infused my energy. I began to cut quickly and close to my head. I did not stop until it was all gone and less than an inch remained, as I was convinced it was new growth.

I stared at the large pile of hair surrounding my feet and wept.

Chapter 82

I knew that I would have to reach for MJ at some point, but not yet. I couldn't formulate a way to apologize, and begin to make up for the damage I'd done by not believing her. I only hoped that when I did reach, she would speak to me. The next few days were a blur of memories and realizations. With each memory the anxiety climbed, and sleepless nights plagued me.

Dr. Braun had spoken to Dr. Ashton and explained my chemical imbalance. She agreed to keep me on his prescriptions, as we were handling the mercury and working on healing my spine.

My thoughts ran overtime and the memories came back in splinters initially, then in a flood. With each passing moment, the magnitude of the betrayal settled deep within my being. I finally accepted that Mark was trying to kill me. But I spent hours obsessing on *why*? We had lost all the money in the company, including my own – what did he have to gain?

I took to wandering the plaza to try and piece the puzzle together. A small sign for life insurance made me stop in my tracks. It sparked the memory of two life insurance policies that were held both personally and in the company. They had double indemnity clauses, and would have made him a very wealthy man. His transformation had been complete, and right after the wedding, when all the papers were signed and the beneficiary declared.

How could I have been so foolish? I stood in the hot sun with the memory saturating my psyche. I felt the desert heat burning my shoulders, and knew it had been a prolonged period. When I finally stirred, I saw a group of Pueblo woman looking at me with alarm. I must have stood like a terror struck mannequin. I shuffled away quickly as I didn't want to engage anyone.

Thoughts were racing wildly as I tried to make sense of the facts. I thought of all the other lives Mark had also ripped through. How many of the investors lost their resources as he was trying to take mine? What did he bury in the bankruptcy records? What was the document he tried to force me to sign? How many had their fortune wiped out while he was plotting to kill me? Were they just in the way or did I take too long to deteriorate from the noxious coffee?

I recalled the way his lanky build could cross a room in a few steps. How his startling blue eyes could capture me from across a room and I'd be weak in the knees for hours.

I thought of his Southern charm and the way he would thank women with "Yes Ma'am" and men with "Yes Sir." It tricked me into thinking his chivalry was genuine, when instead it was all a ruse.

I shuffled through the desert heat remembering our early dates, the perfect gifts, flowers, the trip to Hawaii. It all flooded back with hidden innuendos and a new awareness. I could see his tender touch as he leaned in to kiss me. He would take my face in his hand and firmly turn my head to look into his eyes. I thought it was so sexy. Now it made my skin prickle in disgust.

How many times had I awoken to find him watching me? His bare chest muscles would be rippling with the slightest movement. I thought his face conveyed the look of gentle reverence. Instead, it was the reflective appreciation of how he would spend the money that softened his expression.

There was no conversation or instant that wasn't carefully scrutinized, as now I knew it was all a lie.

My blood ran cold. I became chilled to the bone and desperately needed a hot bath to warm my body and wash away the horrid memories.

The temperature would continue to plummet before the nightmare was over.

Chapter 83

The therapy with Barbara was in full swing and with the removal of the mercury, came lessening seizures. By the time the treatments were completed, the seizures stopped. They have never returned.

As each day passed without a convulsion, my rage began to rise. I visualized scenarios where I located Mark and either killed him or better yet, made him pay dearly. I would never have thought myself a vengeful woman, but I carried out more horrid acts in my consciousness.

I had to compartmentalize the hatred, as I could feel it interfering with my healing process. I knew the time would come to face it again, but not now. This man had already taken too much from me. I would not let him hinder my healing.

The only way I could move beyond the depravity was to let go of everything connected to him. For me that also meant changing my name. My given name was Anna Marie, but I cringed to think of the way Mark said it. He thought it was elegant and would say it softly, time and again. I wanted a name that represented who I was becoming, and it certainly had nothing to do with my birth name.

I spent hours researching names and finally settled on Alesandra, as it was the Italian pronunciation of Alexandra, which meant strength. I knew it had taken incredible fortitude to survive Mark. Rain signified mercy and grace in the Native American culture, and both were bestowed upon me. Although I didn't formally change my name for years, I began introducing myself as Alesandra immediately.

My spirit began to lighten as the poison drained out of my body. My humor returned and I began playing with Selsie again. She relished having her mom back, and neither of us cared that we were penniless. Our life was simple and I began to have hope again.

I didn't know how I was going to rebuild my existence, but with each passing day that was seizure free, my strength improved. My sleep was still poor but my spine was healing. As my 40th birthday drew near, I began to have dreams for the next decade.

Chapter 84

*T*he morning of my birthday my mom called, as she was the only person who had my new phone number. Santa Fe was about healing, and I didn't want my life infiltrated by any form of inquisition. There would be time for all that later.

She sang me happy birthday in the sweetest off-tone voice, and I cried tears of joy.

As the day drew on, thoughts of MJ filtered in. I wondered what she was doing for her birthday. We had always spent our special day together and the loss of her was deeply felt, especially at the beginning of a new decade. I imagined her blowing out the candles and opening little gifts while filled with glee. I missed her to my core but just wasn't ready to face her. I needed more strength to address my duplicity.

At dusk the woman from *Kitchen Angels* appeared at my door. Their warm dinners had stopped long before my birthday. But they knew that I was alone in Santa Fe, healing from a major surgery and they baked me a cake, complete with a special message of encouragement in the frosting. It had four large candles and made me cry.

I have received many cakes over the years, but this tiny

confection from thoughtful strangers, will always remain an extraordinary gift.

I made a wish for each candle and envisioned a better year.

Chapter 85

Although I was still on the Effexor, Klonopin and Sinequan, I was off all anti-seizure medication, and in full swing on the reduction from the painkillers when my brother Joe arrived.

He came unannounced and stunned me when I opened the door.

I threw my arms around him, as his presence was a clear indication that my links to life were reconnecting. Then it dawned on me that no one had my address. I pulled back and inquired,

"How did you find me?" I was a bit worried.

"I had to hire a private detective. It wasn't easy!" He said it lightly and I realized he wasn't trying to hurt me.

"Why did you come Joe?" I wanted to hear that he felt bad for what I had endured.

He looked troubled.

"I know you've been through hell, and I'm so sorry I wasn't there for you. But at least now I know why it all happened." He spoke slowly and with great care.

I started to ask another question, but Joe lifted out his

briefcase and pulled out a large folder. My heart dropped to the floor as the name on it was Mark Young.

Over the next two hours Joe proceeded to pull document after document from his file, and my chest constricted further with each. It outlined the history of the man I once called my husband. Two felony convictions for fraud stopped my breathing momentarily. There were many counts in the indictment, but Mark had accepted a plea bargain.

He had moved from New Mexico to Texas, through Colorado and into California, where he found me. In his wake he left hundreds of people destitute. The list of complaints included Conspiracy, Larceny, Grand Theft, Misrepresentation, Pyramid Schemes and Real Estate Fraud.

There was an investigative report from a private detective that outlined decades of multiple identities, failed corporations, marriages, and a trail of destruction. I was the last in a very long line of deceptions. Somehow I didn't feel so special anymore.

Chapter 86

I saw one woman named Connie that was married to him before me. She lost everything and suffered a complete nervous breakdown. It didn't say if she ever recovered.

Kathy's name nearly jumped off the page. It represented years of financial losses and real estate scams. She never married him as she was already married. I wonder how she explained the huge debt to her husband. He left her just as she was on the verge of bankruptcy – and found me. Why didn't I listen to my mom?

The woman he targeted after me was a diplomat's daughter. He started seeing her while we were still married. I remembered the special care he took with his appearance and knew this was the woman. Within six months she had deeded him onto her home. My heart sank for her. I wondered if she was still in his clutch or if he had already ravaged her world and moved on.

With each piece of information all the lies came back in droves. It felt as if my lungs could not draw in enough air. He didn't play ball for the Milwaukee Brewers. Instead he was in the Minor Leagues for only a summer.

I thought of his heartfelt pitch on the bridge in Balboa Park when he proposed. He claimed that he had never had a successful corporation. Not only did he own dozens of corporations in different States, but also he had managed to throw them all into bankruptcy.

That was his modus operandi, driving companies into bankruptcy in order to cover his deceptions. He wasn't after only the life insurance. There was no telling how much money he got away with.

I remembered the call I overheard regarding offshore accounts. Is that where he hid his bounty?

How did I not see his duplicity? Was he just that good an actor, or was I too willing to believe there was such a thing as a *perfect man*?

I told Joe about the high levels of mercury and the fact that we could never prove Mark did it. Joe was well aware of MJ's claims and also suspected the poison originated with him.

Mark used multiple Trust Deeds to inflate properties and cheat thousands of unsuspecting fools. I remembered the multitude of documents I signed without questioning him. I finally realized the magnitude of his con. Where was all the money? Millions and millions of dollars jumped off the page, with everyone in his wake destroyed. I now understood the relevance of an offshore account.

Chapter 87

I set the file down and just looked at Joe with tears in my eyes.

"Why did you come?"

"Because the investors want to stop him and they need your help. They asked me to find you to see if you would testify against him." He said it softly.

The years of deception, pain and loss gave me a deep determination. I didn't want another person to suffer at his hands as I had.

"What do you want me to do?"

A plan was outlined that meant I would have to return to San Diego to testify over the next year while civil and criminal proceedings were underway. The investors were privy to Mark's history and they were circling to attack. But they needed my testimony to nail the coffin.

I was overcome with the conviction that I had to stop Mark. He tore through lives and left a trail of annihilation in his wake. I was convinced that he didn't take the millions and leave the country, because he enjoyed the process of obliteration. This was his calling and mine was so stop him.

Chapter 88

I couldn't leave Santa Fe for several months, as my spine could not be subjected to the pressurized cabin of an airplane.

I spent my days walking the small city trying to gain strength. My spine had a long way to heal, but I was determined to recover quickly so that I could help the investors.

It was only a few months since my last seizure, and I was nervous to be subjected to the stress of a civil and criminal trial. I had to prevent Mark from hurting another, but part of me never wanted to lay eyes on him again – except for sentencing. That was a scene I replayed over and again in my mind's eye. I saw the look of shock as he realized his reign of terror was over. That image steeled my resolve.

The remaining months in New Mexico were peaceful, as if my soul knew this would be the last serenity I saw for some time. I watched the Pueblo women selling their jewelry and wondered what life would be like to be so uncomplicated. Mine was so complex.

Joe and I spoke frequently but he did not discuss the

case at length. He talked of his kids and business and tried to pretend our life was normal. I let him cling to the illusion, as we both knew it would end soon.

He arranged for a mover to take my belongings and car back to San Diego. Selsie and I would fly back to the city I swore I'd never return to.

Chapter 89

As the impending deposition date drew near, my angst increased. We were in a holding pattern until my surgeon signed off the travel.

Joe arranged for me to have an attorney in San Diego to protect me during the proceedings, as we both knew Mark would be contentious. I was terrified of facing him again, but my anger and need for revenge overwhelmed any other feeling. Joe was convinced that Mark would try to reach me prior to the deposition, but I thought he was mistaken. The combination of the restraining order and final divorce decree created nasty letters from his attorney. I was sure he would leave me alone, anyway how would he find me?

Mark did in fact telephone a couple of weeks before the deposition. I felt my stomach turn and tighten. A familiar bile rose in my throat.

"Hi Alesandra. It was hard to find you." His voice was light, as if we had recently spoken.

"How did you find me?" My throat was tight and it came out raspy.

"It took longer than I expected." He clearly wasn't

going to give up his source.

"What do you want?" I spat the words out.

"Listen, we can help each other. I don't know if you are aware that some greedy investors are trying to make trouble for both of us." He was into another sales pitch. I could envision him pacing the floor.

I let my chest constrict but did not hang up.

"It is best if we both keep our story straight. Do you understand?"

He was pushing a bit too hard and I felt his panic. It bolstered my determination.

"What did you have in mind?" I tried to keep my voice light.

"Well, what if we both pled the Fifth during the deposition?" Just as said it, I had a thought.

"What does that mean?" I tried to sound naive.

"It just means that you don't have to answer anything that could incriminate you, and they can't force you."

"I can't travel because I've had spinal surgery recently. Why don't you plead the Fifth. I'll just stay in Santa Fe. Can they make me come back?" I tried to sound scared.

"No – that's perfect. They'll leave you alone. OK, great. Take care of yourself then." He hung up happy.

It was such a typical Mark conversation. He got what he needed and cut the line.

I called Joe and told him that Mark was going to plead the Fifth and refuse all questions other than his name. I told him not to schedule my deposition until after Mark gave his. That way we could have him on record refusing questions. We were both amused at the turn of events and hung up.

For the first time since discovering the poison I thought there was a chance to turn the tide. It seemed plausible that the investors could regain some of their losses and I could get even. We had to stop him before he ran.

I had no idea how it would all play out, but I prayed the gods would be guiding the events that would unfold in San Diego.

Chapter 90

My last few days in Santa Fe were spent packing and preparing Selsie for the journey back to California. Joe located a small apartment that would safeguard me during the proceedings. After it was over I would decide where to go, as I had no intention of remaining in San Diego. The city was synonymous with suffering, and I knew it would be impossible to stay.

Shortly before leaving New Mexico, I received notification that my Federal Disability claim was approved, reminding me of the tenuous state of my health over the past five years. Disability from the State of California was minimal, but Federal Disability would provide enough money to pay my rent – a far cry from what I had when I left San Diego.

But I was still a long way from re-engaging the workplace. My body was weak and my mind was hazy. I attributed it to the years of seizure activity, and wondered how long it would take for my brain chemistry to restore.

I just prayed the upcoming strain would not trigger a convulsion.

Chapter 91

*T*rue to his promise, Mark went into his deposition and pled the Fifth. The attorneys were lined up and ready to fire questions, but Mark would not even answer, "*What is your name?*" Clearly the years of forged identities left him exposed regardless of his answer.

Joe was told by one of the attorneys that Mark left the deposition arrogant and expressed amusement on his way out of the room. He thought he was free.

The next morning my deposition was scheduled for the following week and all parties were notified. I chose to not answer my phone again while in Santa Fe. My mom and brother knew to ring once and call right back, so I'd know it was them. I couldn't risk another encounter with Mark. I didn't have an answering machine or voicemail, so there was no chance a cryptic message would slip through. I would be leaving in a few days anyway.

Mark now knew I was an adversary and would never make that grave an error again. The remainder of the proceedings would be full of clever maneuvers. He was the master of this game, but I was hoping that this time he would be out matched.

At least it was on record that Mark refused to testify. He had given up his one chance to defend himself, unless of course he let the trial go to a jury. Somehow I didn't think he would take such a risk, as his previous convictions clearly indicated that he preferred to plea bargain. Juries were risky and unpredictable. Mark would never leave his fate in the hands of a jury. He preferred to be in control rather than a victim of chance.

Chapter 92

Early on a Friday morning in February 1998, Selsie and I flew to San Diego. I thought about MJ the entire trip, and called her the second we landed. She answered her office phone on the first ring and for a split second, my resolve faltered.

"MJ, it's me. Please don't hang up. I am so sorry!" It came out in a rush of emotion.

"I'd never hang up – I've been waiting for you to call!"

And just like that, I had my twin back. We agreed to meet for dinner in La Jolla for dinner.

I picked up the rental car that Joe arranged, and drove to my new apartment where an air mattress and other items of necessity waited. Selsie expressed her discontent at being hauled in a cage. I comforted her and introduced the new digs – she seemed pleased.

I showered and nervously paced until I couldn't take it any longer. I drove to La Jolla hours early and walked on the beach, gathering my thoughts and reflecting on how much had transpired in the last few years since I saw MJ.

She was waiting in front of the restaurant and I rushed up and held onto her for the longest time. We were both crying and talking together as if no time had passed. Our mysterious twin connection had returned. We began sharing thoughts and knew instinctively what the other felt. I was so happy to have her back in my life.

We spent many hours talking, walking and processing everything that happened. Joe had shown MJ the documents and she wasn't surprised, as her suspicions had been confirmed. She expressed her anger and hurt over my shutting her out. I apologized time and again – there was no excuse.

Eventually her resentment was gone and we looked to the future - to stopping Mark.

Alesandra Rain

Chapter 93

Joe had arranged for me to meet with my attorney a couple of days before the deposition. Bob Feins was a tall, well-dressed man in his mid-fifties, who had an excellent reputation within the legal community. He was a criminal attorney, which concerned me a bit, but I was reassured that he was only hired to protect me. The question, protect me from what, should have crossed my mind. Instead, I thought everyone saw the obvious in Mark. I couldn't have been more misguided.

My first sense of Bob Feins was that he didn't believe me, but instead, thought I was culpable as Mark. I chalked it up to a jaded legal experience.

I should have listened to that little voice but instead, I prepared for the deposition with total self-assurance.

•   •   •

I had scheduled an appointment with Dr. Braun, and we discussed at length the mercury poison and spinal surgery. I asked if we could begin cutting down the medication he was prescribing, but he encouraged me to stay at the current doses until after the legal issues were finished. He was worried what the stress would bring.

His concern had validity and I refilled the prescriptions, thinking my life was making a comeback.

Now that the seizures were gone, it was easier to differentiate the side effects of the drugs prescribed by Dr. Braun. My eyes were horribly sensitive to sunlight often requiring dark glasses, even on cloudy days. My ears had a constant high-pitched ringing that became unbearable at night. Only a loud sound soother washed out the noise in my head.

My world felt dull, as if a blanket was between every life experience and me. However, considering the magnitude of my testimony against Mark, I thought Dr. Braun might be prudent in holding the current medications until the legalities were over and my life again became my own.

Chapter 94

I gave my deposition to a room bursting with attorneys. They could smell blood and each wanted a piece of the action. A civil action was pending with high hopes of a huge settlement.

Bob Feins wasn't present, and instead sent a junior associate who did not say one word during the entire process. I had never been in a deposition before, and therefore didn't question his silence.

Countless documents were delivered and I was interrogated at length about both Mark's involvement and mine. I was shocked at the sheer volume of paper that held my signature. I remembered very few but tried to answer as honestly as possible.

After a grueling five hours, it was over. I felt it went well but had a nagging feeling. The following day I knew why.

Chapter 95

Bob Feins called and asked me to meet with him. I went to his office and waited until he was available. Finally I was led into his sanctuary and the door was closed. His jaw was set.

"I've got some troubling news," he began.

"What?" My heart sank. *Did Mark slip away again?*

"We have until the end of the day to have you booked on felony charges." He was staring hard at me.

"What?" I couldn't think of anything else to say.

"You were the President and CEO of the company and therefore are culpable for the losses."

I couldn't believe my ears. There had to be some mistake. How could this be happening? I thought we were trying to stop him!

"What are the charges? Am I going to jail?" I was trembling.

"Multiple counts of fraud, diversion of construction funds and grand theft. I'll have you released on your on recognizance." He was so hard.

"Why?"

"Because you are responsible, and it will help in court if you show some remorse."

"Huh?"

"Don't play ignorant Alesandra. I can't help you if you don't tell me the truth. Nobody believes you, even your older sister wrote a damaging letter to the DA. How the hell am I supposed to believe you when even members of your family don't?"

My older sister – a greedy woman who seized an opportunity to make what she thought would be easy money. She had lived her life in pursuit of manipulation and had become a master at the game. Yes, she lost money – we all did. But when the truth about Mark was revealed, she saw a clever way to appear cheated in order to file a lawsuit. Rather than help me stop Mark, it became more important for her to rewrite history and attempt to claim millions against the title company.

At first I thought that Joe had betrayed me and brought me back to San Diego under false pretenses. Quickly I realized that he was duped just as I had been. He was used to convince me to return to testify, while my older sister worked behind the scenes to build a case that would extract as much money from a civil suit as possible. Both MJ and Joe had exchanged heated words with her over the voracity of her greed.

I knew it was all over.

Chapter 96

I was booked, fingerprinted and released later that day. The world had shifted again and I was completely confused. The hope of stopping Mark became a race to protect myself.

Each day I copiously expected Feins and the District Attorney to realize the truth and shift the focus back to Mark, but instead, it brought more confusion and terror.

I finally understood Mark's careful positioning within the company. Although he was charged with multiple crimes, the fact that he was not the President and CEO gave him a certain protection. He was an underling. I was the kingpin. He learned well from the mistakes he made in the past.

My education on the legal process was jaded from the onset. Impartiality in our court system dictated that Mark's two felony convictions could not be used against him, and therefore we both appeared in the arraignment, felony deposition and preliminary hearing as if we were equal – first time offenders.

He had completed his probation and therefore his true history was stricken from the record. Mark could afford an attorney that would fight for him. I on the other hand had an attorney that just didn't believe me.

Chapter 97

$\mathcal{T}$he arraignment hearing was the first court appearance. All that is required is to enter a plea of either guilty or not guilty, and then another court date is set to either go to trial or to establish the sentence.

Mark stood in front of the judge looking like the innocent boy scout. I wanted to scream but had to maintain my silence, or be found in contempt of court.

I watched the dance that emerged in the courtroom and began to comprehend the skill of my adversary. Mark relished the legal maneuvering, as he had always prevailed in the past. He had no reason to believe this outcome would be any different.

Before long my hope was to remain out of prison and even that was looking doubtful.

I was caught in a world of jaded jurisdiction, against the man who had entrapped me. I was viewed as a co-conspirator in the crime of fraud, diversion of funds and grand theft.

MJ stood by me through it all. We saw each other nearly every night and tried to keep conversations light and hopeful.

My anxiety soared and sleepless nights became the norm. Once again, my world was crumbling.

Chapter 98

After a plea of not guilty, which is the standard response for the first court appearance, Feins called me into his office to meet with him. I knew it would not be pleasant, as his attitude had continually declined. He thought I was guilty and would not even consider an alternative.

Although the not-guilty plea stood on record, it did not mean that he would protect me in court. It was only a cursory declaration that had to either be proven at trial, or reversed in the next court appearance.

Feins had met with the District Attorney and had a tentative deal on the table. If I reversed my non-guilty to a guilty plea, then I could be spared the expense and time of going to trial. If I went to trial, the cost would be astronomical and if I lost, the sentencing guidelines would be more severe, with no chance to negotiate the sentence.

Feins wanted me to plea guilty to one count of diversion of construction funds, as Mark had already agreed to plea to one count of grand theft. I felt boxed in.

I wanted nothing more than to scream and fight, but I

knew this was a losing proposition. Feins wanted to wrap it up as quickly as possible, close the file and move on to his next target. I was a nuisance.

I called MJ and discussed my options. We both knew that it was over. I didn't have the money to defend myself, and the District Attorney refused to separate my case from Mark's. I would have to help Mark at a trial if I wanted to fight for my innocence. That was clearly not an option.

I decided to accept the plea and try to move on with my life. We would both be awaiting sentencing guidelines.

I've heard stories of the failure within our justice system but always doubted the validity – until I was caught in the trap.

My one speeding ticket never prepared me for the intricacies of the game of justice. It is truly a chess match and the more you play, the better your odds of navigating it correctly.

Mark was a master and seemed to move with ease. At each court appearance he looked rested and not the slightest bit concerned. I was the only one with dark pillows under my eyes.

I was losing the game and he relished in the victory.

Chapter 99

*A*midst the legal proceedings, I decided to retrieve the boxes that I had stored at my friend's house before moving to Santa Fe. I needed something to focus my attention on, as I was waiting for an appointment with the probation department later that week. After the interview was conducted, a recommendation would be given to the court. They would either view me as a good candidate for probation or recommend prison. Both would mean a felony conviction.

I dragged the boxes back to my apartment and began rifling through them, not looking for anything in particular. I shuffled through boxes of company files but nothing offered any new information – most had been used in the deposition.

A few boxes stood out from the rest – they were labeled in Mark's handwriting in black marker. *Tax Files, New Mexico* and *Personal* peaked my interest. I opened the first box and found what appeared to be files of real estate deals dating back years. They were a boring compilation of real estate documents. Just as I was convinced there was nothing significant in the box, a little note fell from a folder. It was written in Mark's angry hand:

> *Humiliating*
> *Degrading*
> *Embarassing*
> *Incompetence of Counsel*

My heart skipped a beat as I saw historical evidence of his deranged ranting. This was evidence the court would never have, as it was Mark's personal documentation through each scam. Each file held cases I never saw in the report that Joe brought to Santa Fe. I had no idea if any of the information had been used in his previous convictions, but my suspicion was that I was looking at his private mementos. The rest of us kept photo albums, he kept verification of his dishonesty.

I wanted to put it away as it was painful to see proof of his lunacy. But something made me look through the file more carefully. It was not just any real estate file, but rather a blueprint of how he cheated this man. The entire paper trail was in the file, including every Trust Deed and Promissory Note.

Closer inspection of the box revealed dozens of files. It was bursting with lists of banks, couples and individuals that Mark had conned. They dated back twenty-five years, and with each passing year he became more skilled. The files had handwritten notes of congratulations or criticisms – to himself.

But in the early 1980's, Mark discovered a wealth of untapped cons - women. The files then shifted and became a grouping of various women – New Mexico, Colorado, Texas. Each had histories, descriptions of personal preferences and then the inevitable paper trail as he eviscerated their worlds.

I telephoned MJ and she came right over. We spent the night riffling through the boxes, both amazed at what we were witnessing. Contained in the boxes were decades of fraud and mementos of each victim.

Then I saw my name.

Chapter 100

*I*t was a newer file with my name neatly scrawled across the tab. I must have gasped, because MJ moved from across the room and was instantly sitting next to me, having abandoned the file she was examining. We began to slowly view my life – my accident, education, financials, family history, zoological membership, credit card statements with highlighted restaurants and stage tickets, credit report and stock portfolio breakdown. The handwritten notes included:

Entrepreneur
History of Depression / Injuries
Married Twice
Wild Animal Park
Jeans
Auto Accident at 19

The reality of the deceit slammed my stomach further into the floor. How was this possible? How did he get this information?

I shifted the folder and a letter fell out and hit the floor.

I reached for it with trepidation, knowing anything was possible.

It was a letter from Mark's ex Kathy, that she had written to me years ago, yet I'd never laid eyes on until this moment. I began to tremble as I read it.

Dear Alesandra,

I don⊞ know you and you don⊞ know me. I would like to warn you to be very careful. You are on an accelerated downward ⊡nancial spiral and you are not even aware of it. Mark has been perfecting his skills over the past ⊡fteen years and has become much more dangerous. Get away from this man before he destroys you. He is in a serious game with you as you have much more money than the rest of us did. Save Yourself! If you stay, I just hope and pray you have the strength to survive it.
Kathy

I couldn't breath after reading it. MJ held me as the magnitude of the malevolence shrouded the room.

Chapter 101

My appointment with the probation department was with a kind woman named Karen, who belied the power she held. She went through all the charges at length and questioned me on various points. She asked about my history in business as well as my schooling. At the end of the interview she asked very simply why I became involved in a real estate scam?

I remembered the way Feins drilled me on the interview. *Do not give any facts about Mark; accept responsibility and leave.* Yet something made me trust this woman. I hesitated and then decided to follow my own guide.

I proceeded to tell her about Mark's files, including the letter from Kathy. I even shared the hair analysis report and asked her to please look into Mark's past. I told her that the issue wasn't if I was convicted, it was if Mark walked away and was allowed to do this to yet another person.

Karen asked if I could compile a brief, and bring it to her in a couple of days outlining a few of the files I located. She asked me to not include anything on myself and write the document in third person. She said to include any supporting records.

I spent the next forty-eight hours examining files and writing the brief as she asked. It was a complicated and exhausting effort, but at the end of day two there were 89 supporting documents with 46 examples spanning nearly 20 years. I discovered a total of 14 fictitious names that Mark had used, including social security numbers and bank accounts.

I delivered the work to Karen. She stated the documents would be authenticated and that she'd be in touch. Within ten days she called and asked me to come to her office. She had a look on her face I could not read. Karen told me that her investigators had verified the documents were authentic, but they could not be introduced into evidence, as it would be prejudicial against Mark in the sentencing phase.

I was about to debate her when she said very quietly,

"I want your sister to deliver the envelope to the judge who is presiding over sentencing."

"How? I don't know his chamber." I spoke just as softly.

Karen handed me back the large envelope and reached for a pen. She scribbled the Judge's name, chamber and case reference on the outside. Then she smiled.

Chapter 102

Criminal proceedings protect the rights of the defendant and although extensive documentation was provided, it could not be admitted into evidence, without a little help.

MJ delivered the envelope to the judge's bailiff but we had no way of knowing if it was reviewed or discarded. The sentencing hearing was drawing near and as it did, my anxiety continued to climb.

I saw Dr. Braun before the hearing and he suggested we increase the medication. I declined, as I wanted my senses as sharp as possible for what was coming. He was not happy with my choice but said he would see me after the sentence was issued. If I needed an increase, I could call him.

The day before sentencing I was completely out of body. MJ stayed with me and we drove to the court together. Feins met me outside the courtroom without any indication that he had changed his mind about me. He was already done representing me. It was a formality to complete this final stage.

Chapter 103

*I*t all became surreal – the facts remain a blur. I remember floating into the courtroom in a state of high-anxiety.
My feet were full of lead and my head was light. It was hard to
concentrate.

Feins had warned me of very little. I glanced around
the courtroom and took in the players. A judge ruled from his
raised bench. It was more intimidating than anything I had ever
seen on television. The court reporter had a bored look on her
sad face, as if there was nothing surprising in her dim little
world. The attorneys talked amongst themselves – clearly a
club that allowed only private membership.

The galley of prisoners was the most fearful – men
dressed in orange jumpsuits, most handcuffed. Their looks of
boredom and disgust frightened me. They did not seem of this
world – at least not the world that I knew. It all came rushing in
a wave of terror. Somehow the magnitude of what was facing
me came crashing down over my senses.

I looked around the room. Faces, smiles, scowls, they
all rolled together. I could not hear voices, only the panic of my

heart slamming in my chest cavity. I glanced at MJ. She had a forced look of calm but her large almond eyes showed too much white space. Her panic was rising as well.

Then I glanced at Mark. Who was this man who stood with such confidence? He was laughing with his attorney, clearly composed over the situation at hand. He was in the middle of an amusing anecdote and was drawing out the punch line. I wanted to pummel him.

He looked so foreign. As if we had never been introduced. It was clear he hadn't lost a night's sleep. His hair was perfectly combed back and his business suit was immaculate. He had a fresh manicure and his shoes were spit shined. He stood with total confidence, as if he knew he was championing a victory.

I wondered how anyone could prance through life without a conscience. It puzzled me and infuriated my sense of morals. I speculated that all his previous victims held the same indignation. At first filled with the hope that you could foil his conquest, and then the awareness crashing, that makes it obvious the flagrant gaps in our justice system could set him free. It was all a game, and unfortunately he was winning.

Chapter 104

The anticipation of not knowing whether the presiding judge had read the file was killing me. I started the day a free woman, but how would it end? My heartbeat was too fast for my frame, and I could not feel my body. Was this normal?

I had nothing to compare my experience in the criminal justice system to but traffic court – hardly a fair comparison.

This time my entire future was pending on the interpretation of the judge. Would he differentiate between Mark and me? Or would I be viewed just as evil and rot in a prison somewhere? Was this gamble worth the outcome? I had no idea. What drove me through the legalities was the prospect of stopping him. Could it possibly happen today?

The bailiff had announced the judge's arrival and he entered the courtroom with a fierce look on his face. My determination faltered and I wanted to run – it was too late.

Judge Harris took his seat on the towering bench. He dropped a stack of folders and began to rifle through them. Eventually he located his trophy and held up a tattered manila envelope as if it was full of hot coals. My stomach rolled over.

I wanted to look back at MJ but didn't dare move. It was the package she had delivered to his chambers, and it had clearly been worked through. He had read it - that was certain. And he looked furious. The day looked brighter but my body belied the possibility of justice.

Judge Harris spoke between clenched teeth.

"We are here to issue the sentence to both of these defendants. Some information has been delivered to my chambers and I want it introduced into evidence!" He spoke with a fierce quality that made me stop breathing.

He lifted the parcel as he spoke, and I watched him raise it and lower it, over and over again. I lost the rhythm of his speech until he addressed my attorney.

"Represent her!" Was all I caught, but it sounded like a scolding. Oh my god, he saw the truth.

Then Judge Harris turned to the District Attorney and commanded, "I want this entered into evidence. I want to rule on the totality of information available to me. I'm going to take a 15-minute recess for you to decide."

With that he left the courtroom.

Chapter 105

Pandemonium broke in the courtroom. I was still glued to the floor. The bailiff brought the envelope down for the District Attorney to review. He opened it carefully but there wasn't sufficient time to inspect in detail. He read a few lines of the brief and stopped.

Mark shifted his position to see the evidence. His eyes flared, it was the first time he showed anything but complete confidence. He flashed a look of absolute hatred that sent shivers up my spine. I saw his true nature for a split second and it was frightening. The polished man was gone and the demon lingered.

The world seemed to stop as my attorney joined in the little group. I finally turned back and looked at MJ - her eyes were full of excitement. She didn't blink, just held my look with wide saucers filling her face. It was a pivotal moment - we were so close. This evidence could send him away for the full 5 years. I tried not to show emotion. Unfortunately, Mark had a rapid recovery and regained his arrogance.

He turned to face the DA and with complete bravado he stated simply, "If you allow this into evidence, I'll retract my plea and we'll go to trial. I'll tie you up for years in court and I'll win, because I'm smarter. Accept my plea the way it stands."

The District Attorney was used to playing this game and therefore didn't show any exasperation as I had hoped. He seemed to evaluate the situation quickly and didn't say a word. He went back to his table and spoke quietly to the Assistant DA. Then the Judge re-entered the courtroom and it became deathly silent.

"Well, what is your decision?" He looked straight at the District Attorney.

"We want to exclude the new evidence and proceed with sentencing as planned."

I stopped breathing. Inwardly I was screaming NO! Outwardly I felt faint and rocked on my feet. The Judge hesitated for a brief moment, then did the only thing he had the power to do.

"I cannot rule on this case now that I have all the evidence. I will not sentence this man to only probation. Therefore I recuse myself from this case. You will be sent to a new courtroom."

He slammed the gavel down and in a flurry of robes - he left.

"What does that mean?" I asked Feins.

He looked furious at me.

"It means he is stepping down. We will be issued a new judge."

"Can he do that?" *What had we done?*

"He saw information that was prejudicial and now he can't rule. What did you and your sister do?"

MJ walked up to us and Feins couldn't contain his irritation, "I'm trying to do heart surgery and you two are doing a liver transplant!" He stomped off.

Neither of us said a word.

222

Chapter 106

*T*he following day we went back to same court, new judge. This time the file had been sanitized before he ruled.

It was over in a matter of moments. I received two years probation on one felony count of Diversion of Construction Funds, and Mark received a felony conviction for Grand Theft. He was sentenced to six months work furlough at a low security installation – meaning he could spend the week a free man and go to jail on the weekends. He was also given a probation term of five years. We were both liable for a restitution order in the amount of $300,000, accruing at 10% per year.

I remembered all the documents from his previous convictions. While on probation he continued to con people. As long as he was free to walk the streets he would resume his destruction. This ruling was a total failure.

Mark strutted down the aisle of the courtroom with a smirk. He threw the door open and flung it against the wall. I heard it crack. No one stopped him. He was proud and I was overwhelmed with the sensation that I would forever be trapped.

I left the court proceedings feeling it was all for naught. Mark escaped and now in 1998, just seven years after meeting him - I was a convicted felon. He had a third conviction and was still granted liberty. How was this Justice?

●   ●   ●

My disillusionment and hopelessness pervaded every waking moment. I would begin each day with the realization that I was now a felon. The despair only deepened as the days progressed.

I had failed in the worst way. Although many of the investors had filed a civil suit to recover their money, some had lost everything, as I had. I didn't know if they would be able to recover any money or how much.

And what about the unsuspecting public that Mark would continue to prey on? There was no doubt he would keep on cheating, as he fed on manipulation and the conquest.

It wasn't just about the money or he would have left the country before the court ruling. He enjoyed the game and knew there was still too much to be skimmed in the states.

What I also knew was that I would never regain my standing in society. The fact that he poisoned me would never be unearthed. I was sure that he would do it again.

Chapter 107

Each time I saw Dr. Braun he discussed increasing my medications. I just desperately needed to talk about the whole debacle with Mark. Instead, he would rush me through the appointment as my designated 15 minutes were up. I would leave feeling wounded with my prescriptions in hand.

Melissa no longer lived in the area and I just couldn't face trying to find another therapist. I chose to hold my thoughts inside.

Dr. Braun continued to push and I finally acquiesced and accepted the increase. I felt numb – it was a welcome respite.

I could not leave San Diego for the next two years anyway while I was on probation. It was a horrid feeling of entrapment to be tied to a city that held nothing but anguish, but at least I wasn't in prison.

Even though I was not incarcerated, I had no sensation of freedom. My life had been built on business opportunities and great credit. Who would ever trust a convicted felon? The defeat was overwhelming.

My health no longer seemed the primary importance. In

Santa Fe, I had the strong conviction that if I could regain my physical state then I could reconnect with a new line of work. I thought it was hopeless after the conviction.

Articles about the conviction were printed in the newspaper and covered in detail. One reporter mentioned my seizures, but no one wrote the true story.

Any outing left me feeling exposed. I had a Fourth Waiver that basically meant I could be searched at any time without cause. I was terrified that if I were stopped for a speeding ticket then I would be thrown in jail. Therefore I seldom wandered out as I was convinced the whole world knew about my state within society. I felt crippled.

No one brought up Mark to me. My family kept their discussion to themselves. What was there to say?

My back pain increased and with it the impression that my existence was doomed to remain small.

Chapter 108

MJ had stayed in San Diego and tried to inspire me. She reminded me continually about my drive for a college education – until I lost my world to Mark. She was relentless in helping me find something of value after all the pain I had endured.

Although the surgery in Santa Fe had released the immediate nerve impingement, my spine became tender again. The discs above the original injury began to bulge, and with it came increased pain. Some days were fine and others meant laying on ice to stop the inflammation. My spine felt wobbly, as if it was unsupported by any muscle group. Yet in spite of the waves of discomfort, I did believe that finishing my education could keep my mind off both the present and past. I had always appreciated the process of learning, and felt the diversion could help while I was bound to San Diego.

I enrolled in a local University and spent the next two years completing my bachelors in Psychology. I began to slowly build a tiny group of friends but was careful to tell no one of the conviction.

My pain continued to increase and I finally resorted to

227

having more epidural blocks in an attempt to control the nerve injury. Nothing helped.

I lived a very quiet existence and spent my time focused on my studies. There were days at a time that I would not think of Mark. I could almost forget that he ever touched my world. But every month I had to file a probation report, and it provided a continual reminder of my nemesis.

Selsie was nearing twenty and had slowed considerably. I knew her days were numbered and we spent many hours curled up together while I studied. In the Spring of 1999, she finally died in my arms lying next to her favorite toys. I watched her little body slip away, so grateful for the two decades we had together, and unsure whether I could ever love another animal again.

The pain of her loss left me hollow for weeks, but I knew she held on until she was convinced I had a strong enough lifeline.

Chapter 109

After graduating with honors in 2000, I did an internship in a residential home for schizophrenics prior to entering graduate school, and the experience jaded me on the world of psychiatry.

Tender souls came to the facility after experiencing either auditory or visual hallucinations, and were given massive amounts of anti-psychotic drugs. Eventually the drugs made them shuffle and have strange body tics. They became shells of beings, relegated to an existence without merit. It broke my heart.

I also began to get a glimpse of what my future could hold. I saw how easy it was to become a ward of the state and lose your liberty. Many of the patients begged to come off the drugs and were told they were non-compliant. The staff was kind but would not even consider an alternative method. They were easy to control while on cocktails of drugs. It mattered little that their creativity and ability to communicate was destroyed. They were no longer considered human beings, but rather schizophrenics. And of course, I saw the way the world reacted to these lovely people when we had them on social outings. They skirted away from them, as if their demons were contagious.

It soured my experience in the realm of psychology and the lovely connection I had shared with Melissa. Psychiatry was only about drugging, and I no longer felt that studying about personality disorders reflected my inner truth. It appeared to be more focused on determining the ways in which we were abnormal versus why we were unique.

I left the field of psychology and decided to pursue a Masters in Film Studies. I had never considered the film industry as a career, but it had always fascinated me. The ability to convert the written word to two-dimensional images was enticing. It was also an arena I hoped would not be as critical of my past. There were many in the industry that had jaded pasts and went on to create something of value. I knew it was highly competitive, but hoped I would find my standing.

MJ encouraged me to not think about the future, but just take the present a day at a time. I took her advice to heart and focused my energy in graduate school.

I met a kindred spirit who has been a dear friend over the past five years. Mike helped restore my faith in people, as he never judged me. I eventually shared my story and he reared in anger over the injustice. He was the first person I trusted enough to share my past with. He never questioned my integrity. It was a significant friendship at a critical time and strengthened my belief that I could heal.

About midway through my graduate work my back pain returned in earnest. I was told that my spine was deteriorating – and once again, the cause was unknown. The pain continued to increase and I did not want to end up on powerful painkillers forever.

I watched so many patients in the clinic who spent

their life on strong medications and they seemed to be shells of people. Why were there so many back injuries? They all seemed like average people who had never over-exerted their body. It made me question why a life on drugs was the answer.

I often thought about all the medications that Dr. Braun prescribed. My medicine cabinet relegated an entire shelf to the bottles. He often stated that I had a chemical imbalance, but I wondered how you repaired it. There was never a discussion of stopping the meds or determining what exactly caused the imbalance. He only declared that I would need the meds forever if I wanted to stay stable. I wondered what was wrong with my brain that insomnia haunted me. I couldn't sleep without the Ambien and Restoril and my anxiety would climb if I missed even one dose of the Klonopin. A day without Effexor or Sinequan would leave me crippled with electrical shocks in my head. Every time I brought up my concerns, Dr. Braun would say that *my condition required the medications.* I was perplexed that there wasn't a test for my malady, but I trusted him.

Chapter 110

In 2001, I had a Dorsal Column Stimulator implanted in the hopes of controlling my pain without more drugs. The stimulator is a specialized device that stimulates nerves by tiny electrical impulses via small wires placed on the spinal cord. Basically it interrupts the conduction of pain signals to the brain. The pacemaker used to power the unit was implanted in my upper buttocks. I carried what appeared to be a TV remote to adjust the electrical current. It was incredibly uncomfortable but effective when it worked.

Unfortunately, the device repeatedly failed and had to be re-implanted. Over the year I underwent ten surgeries in an attempt to fix the stimulator correctly, only to be discouraged each time it failed.

The incision up my spine kept growing in size and finally reached 14 inches. I tried to avoid looking at what once was a gorgeous back. My days of modeling seemed like another lifetime.

I just could not determine what my body needed to stay healthy. It was as if the bones were crumbling and could no longer support my weight. A bone scan indicated a significant loss, and as a result calcium supplements were prescribed that only made my stomach hurt.

It was frustrating to have the conquered the seizures only to have my spine deteriorate. I began to wonder if my education would forward my future, as my chance of getting off disability was remote.

Chapter 111

In 2002, my 45th birthday was spent undergoing a hysterectomy due to a large mass in my uterus. I bled for nearly a year before the mass was detected. By the time the surgery was scheduled I was relieved, but extremely fearful of yet another operation. The thought swirled on why my body was continually failing? The idea of future decades filled with ill health left me despondent.

The morning of the surgery, my panic was high. I waited in pre-op for my surgeon, and felt my skin crawling as if bugs had somehow infiltrated the sterile environment.

MJ had accepted a wonderful job in Los Angeles and had moved about six months earlier. She had not accrued any vacation time and therefore could not be in San Diego for my surgery. She had already taken her sick time to be with me during a few of the spinal surgeries. Instead, a friend dropped me off at the hospital and promised to check on me during my recovery.

As they inserted the IV, I could smell the familiar and repulsive scent of anesthesia. I felt the tears drip down my face as the sedative took affect.

I awoke in post-op with the alarms ringing loudly. It took me a few moments to realize they were connected to me. The nurse rushed over and told me to breathe. I remembered thinking *what an odd request,* then drifted back to sleep.

The alarm continued to ring every few moments and it became irritating, as I wanted to sleep. The bells rang through-out the night, as my breathing was so slow the sensors were continually triggered.

The pain was severe and I wanted nothing more than to drift away – far away and not come back.

At what point in the night Selsie visited is unclear. But I awoke to her weight on my chest, just as she had done every day for 20 years. Her little black body was nearly transparent, yet I could feel her entire mass and see directly into her face. She was staring hard into my eyes with a wrinkled forehead – the look Selsie always had when she knew I was in trouble.

I began to cry and told her I wanted to cross over with her – life was just too hard. Selsie opened her mouth to ex-press her discontent but no sound erupted. Her weight became heavier and forced me to breathe. We stayed united until I was safe. Then she drifted away.

I could not understand why she wouldn't let me follow her. Instead I remained connected to life.

•   •   •

One month later I had the stimulator implanted for the last time. It worked for another three months and provided enough relief that I finished the coursework for my Masters at the top of my class.

Chapter 112

I don't know when I decided the medical and psy-chiatric route was failing me, but somewhere deep inside I just knew there had to be a better way. I grew weary of all the drugs, doctors and psychiatric visits. I craved a life that was truly my own. As long as I was tied to the medical community I wasn't really free. It had been nearly ten years since I had been without an antidepressant or tranquilizer in my body. It was four years since the conviction.

The shelf of drugs in my medicine cabinet was a contin-ually reminder of my ill mental health. It read like a pharmacy – Sinequan, Restoril, Ambien, Effexor, Klonopin, Norco and Oxycontin. I wanted to be off them and see how my body and mind would respond.

I scheduled an appointment with Dr. Braun and outlined my hope. He sat with a stiff back behind his desk while the coastline peaked over his shoulder.

He said in the kindest possible tone, "Alesandra, I understand your wish, but you have a chemical imbalance that needs a lifetime of treatment. You have come so far, why push yourself now?"

"For exactly that reason. I've come so far. I want off. How many more drugs are going to be pumped into my body? At some point wouldn't you think they would work? I just can't keep taking thousands of pills a month for the rest of my life. I need to have my life back! Can I just quit them?" I was insistent.

"I think you are making a huge mistake. The medications are the only thing controlling your mood. I think it's best if you thought of them as continuing treatment." He said it with certainty.

"If it was a treatment, then wouldn't I be cured! This cure is stealing my life. I want off Dr. Braun. What do I do?"

"Well, they are not addictive but I would recommend dropping slowly. If all your symptoms return you will have to reconsider your decision." He did not look happy.

"How slowly can I drop them?"

"Well, you can reduce 50% and then bring it down depending on how you feel."

"Great."

I left his office with determination to get off the drugs and get my life back in its entirety, separate from all the doctors. It had been a decade since I had been drug free and I couldn't remember exactly what my mind and body felt like without all the medication.

I had constant headaches, stomach pain, constipation and a horrid dry mouth. My heart continually skipped beats and my hands shook. I couldn't drink water, as it tasted metallic. My nose bled continually and my hand tremors had left me feeling as if I had Parkinson's. My muscles felt stiff and I had aged considerably. I looked closer to 55, but I knew my life hadn't been easy.

The worst symptom was the short-term memory loss. I used to recall numbers at high speed or calculate easily in my head. It had deteriorated to little notes everywhere to remind me of the most basic chores. I was taking nearly two thousand pills a month.

In my heart I had a deep sense that I could have more from life. For the first time, awareness surfaced that I would never attain it as long as I was on the drugs.

Chapter 113

I telephoned MJ that night. She had purchased her
home and was often suggesting I move in with her.

"What would you think about us living together in Los
Angeles?" I hoped she would be in agreement.

"Finally! Yes, that sounds wonderful. When?" MJ answered enthusiastically.

I explained my plan to get off all the medications and
get my body as strong as possible. I had been on disability for
nearly eight years and desperately wanted to be back in the
workforce. The short stint working in the Schizophrenic community was not enough to be considered gainful employment. I
wanted my life back and MJ approved wholeheartedly.

With my coursework completed, all I had left to finish for my masters degree was the comps. The exam could be
taken in Los Angeles.

On January 11, 2003, I moved to Los Angeles to live
with MJ. I was filled with excitement and anticipation over
the prospects of rebuilding my life. I felt a little unsure of my
ability to drive, but I knew that once I arrived at MJ's, I could
completely take care of my health. This was just going to be a

long day.

The movers arrived and began packing up the truck. I left San Diego without regret. I was so finished with this city. The move went without incident and all large items were in place before MJ arrived home.

Chapter 114

I began cutting down on the medications the following morning. I started by reducing the Effexor and Klonopin by 50% as Dr. Braun suggested. I felt a bit shaky but all was well. MJ went to work and I unpacked boxes and rearranged her home.

Everything was tolerable until day three. I awoke in the middle of the night to the worst sense of terror I had ever experienced. Electricity shot through my limbs and I was certain we were in real danger. Then I checked on MJ and she was sound asleep with her cat curled up next to her.

My heart was slamming. What in the world set me off? I remained awake and waited for the answer. It never came. The world around me was quiet, but I had the deepest fear within my body and soul. The hours before daybreak brought increased panic.

By morning I had what felt to be the flu. I was a bit relieved and decided to just ride it out. MJ was her kind and loving self and told me to just relax. She made me tea that I could not drink, and insisted I try and eat a little breakfast. Then she went to work.

Over the next few days the flu-like symptoms became worse, much worse. My body shook and I felt feverish while the nausea escalated to severe cramping. But along with the nausea and fever came increased terror, muddled thoughts and horrid electric shocks ripping through my head.

I tried to step out the front door to get the newspaper but the outside world look terrifying, leaving me petrified to leave the house. The panic brought me to deep sobbing cries as I curled into a fetal position on the floor of the bedroom.
My god, what was happening to me? My pain was soaring and I was feeling very desperate. My back was hurting more than usual and the area around the pacemaker was throbbing.

A telephone call to MJ provided a local doctor who was also an acupuncturist. I called and her nurse asked me to come immediately. I couldn't wait for MJ to get home so I drove to her office with a deep sense that something was desperately wrong. My terror at being out in the open was crushing.

I crossed the tracks for the Metro Link, LA's mass transit train system. A passing thought of a news story entered my mind. This was where a man was hit by a train and killed. The next thought was more terrifying; *if I timed this right I could be out of my misery.*

It threw a blanket of cold fear over my soul. Where the hell had that thought come from? I hadn't had any thoughts of suicide since the nightmare with Mark and the poison. I picked up my pace and drove to the doctor's office.

Chapter 115

Dr. Miaki was a tiny Japanese woman in her mid 70's that dressed in perfect attire. Her hair was wound in a meticulous bun and her white blouse was crisp. She exuded compassion and warmth. Even with my horrid flu, I knew I was in good hands.

She sat down and asked a litany of questions – age, past medical history, current medications, etc. Her eyebrows lifted slightly as I listed the litany of drugs,

"Restoril, Ambien, Klonopin, Sinequan, Effexor, Norco, Oxycontin and Zanaflex." Then I explained how I was determined to get off all of them and had dropped the amount per my psychiatrist's instructions.

She hesitated then said the words that will ring in my ears forever, "This is not the flu. You are in withdrawal. Valium class drugs are very addictive. In fact, my brother and I will not dispense them in our practice. I think you dropped too quickly and that is why you feel so bad."

She said it without invalidation, without judgment. She had a look of deep concern on her face.

I was mortified. "Withdrawal?! I was told these were

non-addictive."

"Well, they are terribly addictive. Would you consider raising the levels back up and bringing them down slower?" She asked with true concern.

"Well, I'd rather not. I really want to get off these Dr. Miaki. Can't I just tough it out? Exactly what class of drug is Valium?" I had the worst feeling in the pit of my being.

"It is a group called Benzodiazepines. Valium was the first and Xanax, Klonopin and others followed." She stopped speaking but it was clear there was so much more behind her statement.

"Why don't you prescribe it?" I asked and felt the world drop out when she answered.

"Because my brother and I read all the early reports of the high suicide rate associated with Valium. We were approached 40 years ago to test the drug on a group of mentally retarded, and we refused. They are not safe." She said it with the slightest hint of anger.

"I had no idea. Well, I'd like to keep withdrawing. I mean, how long could it take?" I had a deep uneasy feeling.

"I commend you for wanting to get off these drugs. Most people stay on them for life. We will need to do blood work and start you on some good vitamins to strengthen your immune system through the withdrawals."

She began to call the nurse to draw blood. She gave me a note to pick up various vitamins then set me up for acupuncture to help with my pain and nervousness.

Chapter 116

I left her office convinced I could push through the withdrawals now that I knew what was happening. I drove back to MJ's and began to research the group of drugs I was given in San Diego. I saw chat rooms filled with people suffering. There were groups for antidepressants, benzodiazepines, even for sleeping pills and painkillers. The horrifying stories made my fear climb as most were on one or two of the meds but no one was taking the cocktail I was.

I wasn't afraid of quitting the painkillers as I had done it many times over the years. It felt like the flu but passed relatively quickly. What scared me were both the antidepressant and the anti-anxiety class drugs. They were the ones that filled the chat rooms with people begging for help.

It was the benzo class that seemed to be the most dangerous. I was on three of them still; Klonopin, Restoril and Ambien. Warnings of strokes and seizures made my terror climb. How could I be prescribed a drug that could actually induce a seizure? After all I had been through with the poisoning, these pills were even more dangerous!

I decided to slow the taper and only reduce one drug at

a time. I chose the Klonopin as it seemed the most perilous. The following morning I broke the tiny pill into four pieces and took three-quarters of the original dose, but I took this same amount four times a day. It seemed a prudent decision.

This is when the nightmare began in earnest. The withdrawals intensified day after day and week after week. A month passed and I was brought to my knees. I became a shell of a woman, full of fear, crying continually.

Unlike the mercury poison, withdrawals from these meds made me feel like I was literally going insane. It wasn't the physical symptoms that were as debilitating, as I had suffered years from surgeries and was use to extreme levels of pain. It was the mental deterioration and irrational thoughts that plagued me continually. I replayed snippets of my marriage with Mark and could not stop the repetitive memories. I felt the anguish with an intensity that was a hundred fold more powerful than the day I lived it. The grief was unfathomable and with it came the electrical shocks accentuating every memory. It was excruciating.

Over the next few weeks I slowly tapered the drugs – a quarter tablet on any one drug at a time. But the withdrawal symptoms continued to intensify. I couldn't sleep. I couldn't eat. I couldn't stand, sit or converse. The days, dragged endlessly.

Nothing provided comfort. A warm bath felt like acid on my skin. The sounds of birds chirping felt like jack hammers. The normal noise within the house felt amplified, as if I was in the middle of a giant earthquake.

And there was MJ. My rock. My lifeline. My sole contact to the outside world. She never faltered in her belief that I could kick this horrible curse.

Chapter 117

I scoured the Internet for any piece of data on antidepressant or benzodiazepine addiction and withdrawal. I located sites from all over the world. The benzo group was primarily in the UK, which only fueled my anger. There wasn't even a chat room that originated in the United States for this class of drugs. Complete strangers from all corners of the globe were reaching for souls who understood their plight.

The chat rooms were full of people who were suffering from these insidious drugs and time and again they asked *why these drugs were legal?* So many couldn't make it through the withdrawals and reinstated the drug to ease the pain. I tried to hold my resolve to find a way through this nightmare.

But as the minutes flowed into endless hours and the days seemed to screech to a halt, I began to question my ability to win. My resolve faltered continually and without MJ's continual nurturing, I would never have made it.

I became convinced that I had done permanent damage to my brain, as all my senses were heightened and painful. All the literature referred to the neurological damage caused by these prescriptions.

Chapter 118

I began to read the stories of those cursed to communicate only through the Internet, as they could not leave their home. Like me, most were prescribed the drugs for basic complaints.

Some couldn't sleep and ended up on a cocktail of drugs for years. Others were in menopause and given antidepressants. One retired minister went to his doctor regarding his poor balance and was prescribed a host of meds that held him captive but never resolved the original complaint.

I was amazed how few actually received the medications from a psychiatrist as I had. Most saw their family practitioner and were entrapped immediately.

I read each story with tears flowing down my face. What was happening to our society that the accepted practice was to drug first? Were the dangers so well concealed that doctors did not realize their cure was actually a curse? I wondered how many doctors were on the drugs and couldn't escape.

The host of side effects to each of the drugs read more like my medical history. The ultimate betrayal came after viewing dozens of postings in chat rooms where other women were stating they also grew uterine masses as a result of being on the meds. How many women have lost their ability to bear children as a result of taking a little pill? Why did any of us ever believe this deception?

This is the largest scam perpetrated on innocent millions. I knew it must be stopped.

Chapter 119

Yet in the thick of my suffering, I felt as if I was in the Lion's mouth without the ability to help myself, let alone another.

Then MJ gave me the words that carried me back to a thread in life. She told me time and again that I had a *special mission*. She told me day in and day out, sometimes dozens of times in the span of a few minutes. She told me how I was chosen to make a difference, and if I gave in and did not get my life back, then they won. I *had* to stay strong and fight.

But day after day MJ watched me cry, not bathe, and crawl on the floor because I couldn't stand. I used to be so particular about my appearance, and yet the withdrawals took any semblance of spirit out of me. I could have cared less if my nails were done or my hair colored. It was all I could do to get through the day without killing myself. I had violent thoughts of hurting myself, MJ or her cat. I became what I'm sure would have meant several other labels by the world of psychiatry, but I knew to keep my distance. I had to heal.

I was completely exhausted without the capability of sleeping more than an hour or two. Food tasted awful and I developed strange cravings. For weeks all I wanted was peanut butter. I ate jar after jar of peanut butter and continued to lose weight. MJ would find remnants on the couch in the morning. I would pass out eating and awake a few minutes later with rushes of panic and anxiety. To this day I cannot eat peanut butter. The cravings from withdrawals have burned the taste from my repertoire.

Many days I could not drive the five minutes to Dr. Miaki's office. MJ would take me after she came home from work. My blood pressure soared. I could hear my heart pounding in my ears and I was desperately short of breath. I became so agoraphobic that leaving the house even to go to the doctor was overwhelming. MJ stood strong through it all.

About six weeks into the withdrawals I developed a serious staph infection in my spinal implant and MJ drove me back and forth to the doctors and the extended hospital admissions to remove the hardware in my body. The infection raced through my body and settled in the bones in my ankle. The pain was excruciating and it was unclear if the infection could be controlled.

Specialists disagreed on whether my heart valve was damaged and required open-heart surgery. IV antibiotics were constant and in-patient hospital stays were necessary to keep the infection from spreading. My body felt like lead – between the withdrawals and infection, my sense of the future grew dim. Through it all I was determined to not increase the meds, but wait until the infection was under control to begin reducing again.

MJ did what I don't think I could have. She was constant. So, when she reached her limit, I knew that I needed help.

Chapter 120

MJ had a caseload of nearly 1000 students that she counseled and it wasn't unusual for her to give special attention, as she is fiercely dedicated. One night she invited about ten students to her home. It seemed a bit strange in light of everything that was happening with me, but I was a guest and certainly not in a position to question her generosity.

I felt better than I had in over a month and was quite the hostess. I kept life stories, served drinks. Overall I thought I was personable and clear headed. Certainly the most sociable I had been through the withdrawal process.

At one point, I remember my sister getting short-tempered with me and I politely pulled her into the hallway and asked her to *please not embarrass me in front of your students.* She left very frustrated and I didn't understand why until the following day.

At dawn I slept a few hours and awoke with the worst hangover feeling and I had not even had a drink. MJ telephoned and sounded tired and completely spent.

"Do you remember last night?" She asked with a

clipped tone I hadn't heard before.

"Sure, it was a really nice evening." My heart was racing furiously and I felt awful.

"Alesandra, there wasn't anyone in the house." She said it flat.

"What?" I was totally confused.

"There wasn't anyone in the house. You were hallucinating. I can't do this anymore."

"Oh my god." My panic flooded every cell in my body.

"This is too scary. You have to call around and find a place to go." She sounded defeated.

I knew what she meant - it was time to find a treatment center. My heart sank. I had pushed MJ past her limit. I had to find a solution, fast.

I spent the remainder of the day researching treatment facilities in Los Angeles. Most used phenol-barbital or other drugs to wean individuals off benzos. No one understood about withdrawals from antidepressants and in fact many used them in their treatment center to help get people off alcohol and narcotics.

They all said how dangerous and painful benzo withdrawals were. My body was toxic and I knew I had to find a facility that could bring me back to a state of health without introducing yet another toxin.

•   •   •

It took hours to locate Cirque Lodge, nestled in the mountains of Sundance, Utah. Their website was full of beauty, including a horse training program. I knew I could heal there.

The telephone yielded a kind, gentle voice. He explained their program, including the costs that were not covered by Medicare. There was no way I could afford it, but it felt like the right place for me. He went on to explain that Medicare might help if I had a referral from my current psychiatrist or doctor.

I telephoned Medicare and was told that drug treatment was not included in my coverage unless I was in physical danger. I needed referrals. I thought both Dr. Braun and Dr. Miaki could provide them without issue. Two should be enough to convince Medicare this was a serious situation. I had an appointment with Dr. Miaki at 5:00 p.m. for acupuncture. I would call Dr. Braun first and then seek Dr. Miaki's help later in the day.

Chapter 121

1 telephoned Dr. Braun, and left a desperate message with his answering service. He returned my call hours later. His voice was cold and clearly he was put off with the tone of my message.

"Hi Alesandra, this is Dr. Braun. What's the problem?"

"Thanks for calling back." I rushed out. "I'm in trouble. I've been working on getting off these drugs. It's been hell. I'm crawling out of my skin and sick as a dog. Now I'm having horrible blackouts. I'm off all but four of the meds and can't do it alone. I need to go to a treatment center, but I can't get any payment from Medicare unless you'll write a letter on the medical danger I'm in. Please!" I was begging and my pitch was shrill.

He responded with a cruel, cold tone. "You are sick because you have an Anxiety Disorder. You need the medication. I can't support you in stopping."

"I'm sick because I'm in withdrawals." I spit the words out. "I've done all the research on benzos and they're dangerous! I want to get off. Please, Help me!"

His answer was flat. "No, I will not support you going

to treatment. There is no need. You have a chemical imbalance and need to take your medication. I will give you the name of another psychiatrist in your area. That is what you need."

I hung up on him and have never heard from him again.

Chapter 122

*L*ater that day at Dr. Miaki's office I proceeded to explain the same situation. I was crying and ended my plea with, "Will you help me?"

"Of course." She said in the warmest possible manner.

"I've always thought what you were doing was commendable but I'm relieved you want to go somewhere safe. I'll write the letter immediately, but Medicare usually has a review committee. It may take months for a response."

I was defeated. "I can't take it anymore. My sister is at her limit. What do I do?"

Dr. Miaki suggested I ask Cirque Lodge if they had any financial assistance for low-income individuals. I left her office a bit encouraged but a little apprehensive. Even treatment wouldn't come easy. It was so damn simple to get these prescriptions but now that I wanted help getting off, there was no where to go. I'm convinced this is one of the avenues used to keep people on for life.

I returned home and called Cirque Lodge again. This time I spoke to another kind soul who explained the scholarship program. I had to write a letter that would be forwarded to the owners. I spent hours composing a letter. I wrote from my heart and requested help. I faxed and mailed the letter and prayed.

The next day I received a return call from Cirque. The management team met and agreed to take me if I paid a minimal amount. For me it was a fortune. I could fly to Salt Lake City and they would have someone meet me in the airport.

Chapter 123

Preparing to leave for Utah took every ounce of energy I could muster. My trepidation was mounting over the thought of flying. I had traveled the world and used to feel completely natural in flight. But what terrified me was the idea of driving to the airport and actually maneuvering through the crowds. I could barely function within the limits of MJ's home, and the idea of navigating through a crowded terminal filled me with dread.

I threw some clothing in a suitcase and tried to steel my nerves for the flight. It was snowing in Utah so I knew that I had to wear shoes and heavier clothing. But the staph infection had left my ankle so painful that all I wore was slippers. I put on a pair of tennis shoes and took the laces out, hoping the pain would be tolerable on the flight. It wasn't.

But it was the blue jeans that had me close to tears. Every nerve ending on my body felt inflamed, and the idea of taking off my pajamas and putting on denim was overwhelming. I knew it would only be a few hours and just prayed I could survive the flight.

MJ piled my bags in the car and came to get me. I sat

on the couch with my arms wrapped around my chest. I had tears in my eyes. She softly touched my shoulder.

"Come on sis. We have to go." Her eyes were so tender.

"Tell me I can make it through this?" I needed her reassurance more than anything.

"You will, I promise." She sat down next to me. "Please remember that you have a special mission. You will beat this and create something wonderful from the experience. Now come on, we have to go."

She stood up and I pulled my shaking body onto my feet. The steps between the living room and the garage felt like a football field.

We had purposely booked the flight late at night to minimize my phobia. I prayed it would be enough. As we drove down the freeway, the headlights from the oncoming traffic felt like lasers. My eyes were running continually, as if I had a terrible infection. I knew it was the withdrawal that was sucking my life force.

I sank deeper into the passenger seat and tried to close my eyes. It was as if my eyelids had a spring sensor that refused to let them shut. I stared at the floor, trying to protect my eyes from the piercing light.

I could feel the movement of the car and my paranoia climbed. The only thing protecting us was a few inches of metal. I could not shake the feeling that we would die in the car, and no matter how I tried, the repetitive thought intensified.

MJ finally got us to the airport and parked the car. She walked me to the terminal. I saw stunned looks as people passed and took in my appearance. My eyes were swollen and my skin was grey. The staples were still in my back from the surgery and I was bent over in pain. The agent at the counter had a concerned expression as she handed me the boarding pass. MJ gave her a soft smile and we proceeded to the security gates where I knew she would have to say goodbye.

She held me for the longest time and kept telling me that I would beat the demon. I didn't believe her, but hung on her words for strength.

I managed to advance through the checkpoint without issue. I sat in the farthest corner of the lounge and called upon the gods to help me get to Utah. It seemed an eternity before I boarded the nearly empty plane.

My seat was in the middle of the plane and too close to the other passengers. A few were watching their TV monitors on the seat back and the images caused throbbing pains in my head. I reseated myself in a quiet section where the screens were dark.

The engines roared in preparation. I clutched the armrests until my knuckles were white. Eventually we were in the air and I sat in fright for the duration of the flight. I popped a couple Klonopin to calm my frayed nerves. As the familiar venom hit my nervous system, I knew they would be the last. I stayed frozen in my seat for the journey and tried to look forward. I couldn't, as I was engulfed with the knowledge that I would soon be in a cold turkey withdrawal. The landing rattled my nerves, but I hung on and knew I was almost at my destination.

I managed to limp off the plane and shuffled toward the baggage claim where I knew someone from Cirque would be waiting. At the bottom of the escalator a gentle face held a small placard. My relief registered across my face. He helped me gather my bags and we began the drive up the mountain. I had made it to Utah. Now the healing could begin.

The check-in process was brief. My photograph was

taken to memorialize my misery. My bags were searched to ensure I did not have any drugs stashed, and then the sympathetic staff showed me to my room.

I could never have been prepared for the horror awaiting me.

Chapter 124

I had already stopped three of the medications before I arrived at Cirque, but went cold turkey on the remaining four the night I arrived. Immediately the withdrawals worsened and I questioned my decision.

Cirque had two facilities, the studio in Provo, Utah where everyone spent a day or two taking tests, filling out forms and acclimating to the center. Then each resident was transferred to the lodge, in the mountains of Sundance. This is where the beauty of the mountain came into play, and where the majority of the healing took place.

My first few days were a blur. I shared a room with a woman I never saw, as I couldn't lie down. My legs shook and twitched uncontrollably. The muscles in my arms fired continually, as if they were both in spasms.

I watched heroin and crystal meth addicts, heavy pot users and those taking painkillers. They stabilized quickly and were transferred to the lodge. I remained in the studio for over two weeks.

Benzodiazepine and antidepressant withdrawal is a beast of a different color and would prove to be the single most difficult accomplishment of my life. Even the horror with Mark, the poisoning, the felony conviction and the 34 surgeries - paled in comparison.

In all the dreadful events of my life I lost portions of myself, albeit for a time. I didn't feel like a whole person. Instead, I was fragmented into tiny pieces that I hoped I could reassemble. I had no connection to these pieces, and very little belief that any sense of normalcy would remain when and if I made it through this nightmare. It was a matter of not only healing physically, but mentally.

I had no connection to the pieces, and very little belief that any sense of normalcy would remain when and if I made it through this nightmare.

For anyone that has done acid, that is the closest way to explain these withdrawals – but you never come down. The hyper vivid colors stay, day in and day out. As the withdrawals deepened and exhaustion built, the alienation intensified. I truly thought I was losing my mind for many endless weeks.

I saw Mark in every dark shadow of the studio. I was convinced he had pursued me and was tormenting my recovery. I could hear his voice full of contempt and his cynical laugh. It would ring through my mind and not stop. His blue eyes would haunt me each time I closed my eyes. They would turn to fiendish pools mocking my attempt at freedom.

I remembered every cruel word he threw at me. Each blow was felt to my core, and I questioned whether I could survive the withdrawals and relive his abuse simultaneously.

I had overwhelming senses of evil, as if it permeated the world. I could feel every sin in my heart – it hurt. I had random images floating into my head as if I was asleep in a vivid dream. They were endless and I couldn't shake them – I feared they would stay forever.

Reality was allusive and chunky, as if I had stepped into a film and couldn't quite fit into a two or three-dimensional world.

I did not sleep for nearly three weeks. When I did, it came in clumsy pieces with tremendous adrenaline flooding my body as I awoke. I could not lie down. My limbs jerked violently. My body was deeply exhausted, yet I could not get comfortable in any position. I cried continually. The beautiful birds that graced the studio in the pre-dawn hours became tormentors. I envisioned snapping their little necks one by one.

The chandelier in the dining room melted and dripped hot molten metal onto my skin. I never said a word for fear they would send me away.

I walked the halls with an arm extended against the wall for support. I couldn't eat. I vomited. Water hurt my skin. When I did shower, I couldn't remember the cycle of my bathing. Did I wash my face first or my hair? How did I hold the soap? My toothbrush looked like an instrument of death. It all became foreign, as if I had never performed the tasks.

The rooms were kept at a constant 72 degrees and yet I was freezing. I wrapped my body in heating blankets and still felt chilled to the bone.

I would look into the mirror and see a reflection that I didn't recognize - as if an old evil woman had crawled in and was mocking me in cruelty. She would mutate into creatures that bore no resemblance to humanity. It was absolutely terrifying.

Chapter 125

*T*he entire staff at Cirque was dedicated and compassionate. They cajoled, encouraged, diligently watched and closely monitored me. A year later, I was told of the endless staff meetings that took place over the danger of my admission. Yet I never knew.

The general manager called me their *Miracle Child* based on the magnitude of my symptoms and my willingness to fight. Their continuous support carried me though every wave of terror.

Each day I was told that I was a day closer. Day in and day out we did this dance of which I felt I gave nothing. I was nearly silent. Words could not be formulated let alone communicated. I was lost to the world.

I was the last resident to kick benzos on site at Cirque. From that point forward, hospital admissions were required at the University of Utah Hospital prior to arriving. In spite of the seriousness of my withdrawals, these kind souls never rushed me and never gave up hope that I would make it. Had they lost belief for one instant I would have sensed it. But their faith was

endless – at times when mine was nonexistent. They let me
draw on their strength and courage until I regained my own.

Group meetings held inordinate pain as the sounds were
amplified. My eyes hurt continually and I took to wearing sunglasses indoors and still suffered tremendous migraines.

I attended every single group session, horse training,
and ropes course, even when my back hurt too much to sit
down quietly. I was determined to find my way back.

I had no idea who I was or what my purpose in the
world would be. I lived only to survive each day and know that
I would not have to live it over.

I did not share my history in its entirety, only my use
of various drugs. My fear of being judged was paramount, as
I thought they would kick me out if they knew I was a felon.

The entire staff gave inordinate attention, but there were
a few special souls that gave me tender care and through their
encouragement, I began to rebuild my lifeline.

There was Shamanic drumming sessions that allowed
me the opportunity to reconnect to aspects of nature. The
rhythmic drumbeats took me to a meditative state where my
mind could escape the racing thoughts of withdrawal. My great
grandmother was Choctaw Indian, and the rich drumming
brought me close to my roots.

As I slowly healed, the colors of the mountain became
rich tones full of promise. Bird songs once again warmed my
soul and no longer tormented. I could smell the sweet mountain air and feel joy. The mountains of Sundance are rich with
animal life, and I longed for the day when I could feel the pull
from nature as I had in my youth.

Chapter 126

*B*ut during my months at Cirque, it was the horse training with Dave Beck that held the closest connection to my inner soul, and became the core from where the healing extended. His rare program provided the most significant link back, not only to myself, but also to others. I learned to trust myself through his unique instruction with these majestic animals.

The horse program involved never actually getting on horseback, but rather was all about personal strength. Each session began with our feeble attempts to put a bridle on the regal creatures. It was intimidating as they were running free in a large pasture, and could not be captured easily. We were taught to use our personal authority rather than trying to overpower their magnitude.

I was so withdrawn from the years with Mark, that I cowered each time the horse approached. I could not use the training rope for fear I would hurt the mare. During one of my early sessions I was close to tears in the large arena. Dave came over to instruct me on the use of the rope. He took one look at the fear in my whole being and revised his approach.

For an hour he had me use the rope on him rather than the horse. His size intimidated me and each time he moved in, I recoiled. I saw Mark charging at me. He would raise his arms to block my instruction, and I saw Mark's fist. I dropped the rope and stood frozen in place. I could not break the memories of Mark's abuse and saw him in the horses and certainly in Dave. I felt paralyzed and unable to comply with the instructions.

Finally Dave stopped the training and started talking to me. He asked he to tell him what had happened to me. I knew it was time to take the risk. I poured out my story in its totality. It was the first time I had shared all the details, including the abuse. Tears poured down my face and Dave just listened calmly while offering nuggets of kindness. Never did he doubt my words or judge me. His humanity enveloped my being and as the hours progressed, I lost sight of Mark.

Dave then told me his story, and how his life had deteriorated on drugs and alcohol. As we stood in the hot sun unfolding our histories, I began to see that I could disclose my past and not be condemned.

Finally we were ready to continue the training. This time I used the rope with steadfast hands. The horse responded and my confidence soared. I found a whole reservoir of untapped power and channeled it into the training. Dave looked like a proud father. I'm sure my smile and determination could be felt throughout the treatment center.

Each lesson was built in layers to expand my ability to set limits. The horses did not care what my past held or whether I had money. They based their response on the clarity of my energy. Dave taught me to trust my strength and courage. He helped me restore boundaries into my realm. I applied each nugget of knowledge and craved more. As the horses responded, I was more willing to carry that lesson to human beings. The memories of Mark began to fade. He no longer crawled out of each shadow or monopolized my day. It was the truest sense of freedom.

Dave provided specific lessons that involved the horses, but also integrated my reserves of personal strength through the written word. I took each writing assignment to heart and would pour my determination into the work. He corrected me with gentle strength and then reinforced each lesson through the horses. It did not take long before the lessons carried from the horses to life. They were readily applicable and I honored each deeply.

All the work at Cirque was significant, but it was the horse training where my heart felt the lightest. I remembered my connection to nature and the familiar pull return began to return in earnest. I never missed a lesson – even 100-degree days couldn't keep me away. My dedication was steadfast and when my time drew to a close, Dave gave me a special graduation. I spent my last lesson sitting bareback with my eyes closed, circling the large arena. I listened to my heart, felt the cadence of the horse and anticipated each movement. The unison was perfect and I danced on horseback through the arena and knew that I had survived.

As a closing gift Dave gave me the training rope I had used over the months. He rolled it up and with pride told me that I had earned it. It was the most significant present I have ever received and to date remains close to me at all times. This simple rope held the journey of over a decade.

Chapter 127

*I*t was well into my second month after being transferred to the lodge that my head began to clear. As my thread
to life became a tether, my humor returned. My laugh is full
and was loved by all the residents and staff. Games like Cra-
nium would leave me in unabridged hysterics. My mind did
not track well enough to provide a correct answer, but it didn't
matter. We all laughed and healed together.

Slowly I realized that it was through the act of reaching toward other addicts from all walks of life, that I found my
calling. I had to give back in some capacity, as helping another
is truly the only way to heal your own heart. It is the act of
kindness that diminishes your own pain and rethreads life.

That is the beauty of treatment. Tortured souls unite
and try to find a way to continue the healing process outside the
walls of detox. It is an amazing experience. I've made friends
I'll have for life.

It didn't matter what our life situation was, or our drug
of choice. Treatment is about mutual healing. About once
again becoming social creatures. Drugs, all drugs, eventually

isolate the human connection. And the more isolated one feels, the stronger the hold of the drug.

We all started using drugs or alcohol to either connect in a social situation, to party, to have fun, or to eliminate pain, depression and anxiety. But eventually the drugs *became* our friends, family and a substitute for accomplishment. They diminished us as beings. We were all here to get back our identities.

These special people, trapped by poisons were exceptionally gifted and tender souls. We were surrounded by kind and committed staff that dedicated their lives to bringing us back to a state of health. Yet we were each told the success rate would be small. Only 3-5% would make it – most relapsed. I looked around the lodge night after night and wondered who would make it. I had to.

Chapter 128

I watched three rounds of residents come and go. We lost some to suicide. I knew two who were suffering from benzo addiction that went out and overdosed. It gave me a clear sense of the travesty facing the world today through prescription drugs.

I watched others leave treatment, as they couldn't take the withdrawals – they were too painful. One man was convinced the intense ringing in his ears could be corrected by surgery. The staff tried without success to change his mind. He left treatment and flew to Los Angeles and straight into surgery.

I saw the results of illegal drugs and how crippled lives became as a result. However, being at Cirque and watching the clutch of addiction was a great equalizer to the magnitude of the prescription drug problem today. How many, like myself, were prescribed drugs without any perception of the dangers?

Awareness began to percolate from a tiny thought into a dream. The seedlings of *Label Me Sane* were planted in this amazing place.

I envisioned an organization that provided support and lectured worldwide on the dangers of all drugs, particularly the psychiatric medications. I also visualized a way to help people in their respective neighborhoods. I had no idea how this would materialize, but I spent hours contemplating my calling. MJ was right. I did have a special mission. Now I had to find a way to bring my dream to fruition.

Toward the end of my stay at Cirque, I became acutely aware of how my past was truly a blessing. There was no way to undo the previous pain I had endured, but if it could be transformed into a fervent passion to help others, well then, it was all worth it.

If Mark hadn't poisoned me, I would never have ended up on a cocktail of medications. Instead, I would have gone on to a new career, oblivious to all those still suffering.

The criminal conviction kept me on the pills and allowed the dependence to grow teeth. And of course, the horrific withdrawals made the magnitude of the issue unavoidable. I also knew the sweetest revenge was to once again succeed. If I spent my life seeking justice against Mark, then he would monopolize my future as well as my past. I knew that I had to recreate something of value. It was my ability to survive the worst in life that could offer liberation.

I remained at Cirque for just under three months and was released with a new lease on life.

•   •   •

MJ drove my car to Utah for family week and then flew back to Los Angeles. I was driving back alone to take the time to assess my future. I sat behind the wheel and remembered my trip with MJ to the airport. I still had some underlying anxiety, but didn't fear the car as I once had. I'm not sure I ever appreciated driving as I did after leaving Cirque.

My greatest fear was still that I couldn't control the pain in my back – and therefore out of necessity, be led back to pills. Although my incision had healed during my months in Utah, the deep nerve pain was still persistent. My joints no longer ached as they once had as they had been inflamed from the medications. It was clearly the spinal injury that still had to be resolved.

My spirit was light – lighter than it had been in decades. I felt like a child again in many ways – full of future promise. My body still felt depleted, but the deep depression that had plagued me for years was gone. The anxiety was tolerable and although my sleep was still fleeting, I couldn't help but wonder why I ever chose drugs as the solution.

As I drove through Utah, a plan was formulated to begin lecturing about both illegal and prescription drugs. I knew the world of legal drugs could be far more dangerous and life threatening, but I was unsure how to convey the information.

I watched the landscape change as I drew closer to Los Angeles, and with each passing mile my resolve strengthened.

Chapter 129

I arrived in Los Angeles with a new lease on life and a new conviction. I was enthused about my new career path, but reality hit me quickly.

MJ's house was full of the memories of withdrawals. She had a gorgeous home, but the rooms were a continual reminder of the old me at a time when my world felt black. I could feel the walls closing in, as if they held the recollections of my suffering and were lingering. I roamed the house remembering the tears, fear and lost hope. But this time I was able to wander out the front door without the agoraphobia gripping my senses. My connection to the world was weak, but it was growing daily.

Even my first shower held the confusion of the nightmare, as I could not determine if my new cycle of bathing was the old Alesandra or a new rhythm I developed at Cirque. It mattered little, as I knew my life would incorporate a fresh style of existence – one that integrated my recovered happiness. The months ahead would be fraught with trials, but somehow I was not frightened. Nothing could compare with the terror I had survived.

My main concern was my health, as it was very weak. My strength felt illusive, as if my body wanted to return to life but it had been down too long. My back hurt continually and I feared I would never recover my strength.

My looks held the lines of ten long years. The wrinkles were deep and prominent and my hair was thin and gray. It was odd that I was not aware of the rapid aging process while in the grips of the drugs. I looked old and worn and certainly had none of the beauty from my youth, but my spirit was hopeful. That was more than I had experienced in a decade.

Chapter 130

I began to research the various categories of psychiatric drugs and the advertising campaigns used to encourage sales. Then I looked for the history of every illegal drug to draw a correlation. The reality made my anger surface. Even heroin and cocaine were at one time legal and used to treat common ailments. Eventually the dangers were discovered and they were outlawed. I wondered how long it would take for the current medications to be banned. I prayed it would be soon, as too many were losing loved ones to this plight.

I spent hundreds of hours building a lecture that could convey the complicated information. I reviewed and added slides as the research poured in. Finally I was ready to test my skills in front of a small group. I needed to assess the lecture module with an audience response to determine if the combination of research and personal experience was effective.

My first lecture was held in MJ's classroom in front of twenty-two students. My stomach was tight and my palms sweaty. I knew I was not ready to disclose my legal past, so I spoke of my multiple operations and addiction to medications. I had to sit on a tall stool, as my back was not strong enough to stand for the hour presentation.

Although the underlying message was received and some students were interested, I had over-complicated the information. Many drifted and began to doodle on their note-books. Others fell asleep. I went back and began to dissect my presentation into easier chunks of information and introduced more visual aids to hold their attention. Then I tested it again.

With each presentation my confidence increased and the lecture inched it's way toward a successful format. Over the months I lectured whenever possible. I had the presentations filmed so I could evaluate my skills. I viewed the tapes I saw my mistakes and realized I had a long way to go before the lecture would affect the audience in a powerful way that could actually inspire.

It was also time to face my inability to pay my medical bills as well as how to resolve the legal ramifications of the restitution order facing me. I still could not sit up for more than an hour comfortably and my immune system was terribly weak. Every cold that came into my vicinity turned into bronchitis in my lungs. It was very discouraging. I was at a loss on how to repair my health and regain gainful employment in order to pay my bills.

Chapter 131

The nagging question that filtered in throughout the day was how to resolve the restitution order and conviction so that I could once again move freely and re-engage the workplace. I had been on Federal disability for nearly nine years and knew the only way to rebuild my life was to use my loss to help inspire others. I could no longer hide from my past, nor did I want a career that meant dismissing what I had endured. I believed to my core that I lived through the nightmare to in turn use my voice to help others.

Yet my poor health restricted my movement and it was a continual frustration to feel my energy wane in a matter of minutes after any small exertion. How was I going to strengthen my body to the point where I could fully engage the world? And more importantly, how would my legal issues stand in my way? The questions were daunting but I held firm to my conviction that my purpose in this world was closely linked to both my survival and ability to overcome all that had transpired.

I wanted to move out of MJ's home to begin my life of independence, but had so many financial obligations as the medical bills were pouring in.

It was an onslaught of creditors. Most were unwilling to work with me in any capacity. I pleaded for terms but time and again I was told to file bankruptcy, as they would prefer to close their books. It didn't take long for me to realize that a second bankruptcy was my only solution.

I contacted every doctor, medical group and hospital and requested payment terms. Each that was willing to work out a payment plan was not included in the bankruptcy. Many refused and were added to the list of dischargeable creditors.

I was deflated but remembered the words of the Cirque staff; *sobriety brings gifts we cannot see.* I prayed that applied to convicted felons.

I searched for an attorney to file the paperwork and made the appointment. I sat in his office and we went through the lengthy stack of medical bills. Then he asked if there were any other bills not listed. I stumbled and muttered something about a restitution order. His eyebrows went up and I proceeded to tell him the story in record time.

He asked how much I paid monthly and I answered, "$25.00."

He became excited and asked if I could bring the paperwork to him as he had a suspicion he wanted to verify.

The last time someone said those words to me I found out about the mercury poisoning. I trotted right home and recovered the file, then retraced my steps back to his office.

Sure enough, at the time of sentencing, the judge's hands were tied on the sentencing guidelines and therefore had to allow Mark probation on a third conviction. But apparently what he *did* have control over was the status of the restitution order.

I'll never know if Judge Harris spoke to the judge that was reassigned to our case, but there was a distinction drawn in how the amount was to be paid, and the court documents determined the limitations on how the massive restitution order applied to our probation status.

Although we were both liable for the $300,000, mine was tied as a *civil judgment* - that meant it was dischargeable in bankruptcy court. It had been a full seven years since Mark and I had filed bankruptcy in San Diego, therefore allowing me a second bankruptcy without breaking the law.

By discharging the restitution order, I would be free of the liability forever. It would default onto Mark to pay as the order was made jointly or severly, meaning that if one didn't pay, it automatically fell to the other.

Because Mark's payment was placed as a condition of his criminal probation, he could never file bankruptcy and discharge the debt. This meant that if he didn't pay, he would be placed in prison for his full five-year term. Mark had often used the bankruptcy courts to bury his criminal actions. This time, the court was placing the restitution order on him without an escape.

As Mark placed primary emphasis on financial gain, this court ruling was a victory – *and I never even knew it*. He may have escaped the jaws of prison, but his movement in this world would be governed by repayment of the restitution order. I felt justice had been served after all.

The day that the bankruptcy was discharged and the restitution abolished, I felt a sense of closure flood my soul. I still held guilt for the investors that would have to depend on Mark paying the debt, but I knew that I was given an opportunity to start over. It was bittersweet as the court did find me responsible, but I truly believed that the judge saw the distinction of our involvement. I would live with the label of felon, but my opportunity to rebuild financially would not be hindered by the massive debt.

After my second bankruptcy, I was totally free.

Chapter 132

My health remained fragile and MJ scheduled multiple appointments with Naturopaths and specialists in the healing arts, trying to find solutions. With each visit I was told I had massive B vitamin and Calcium deficiencies, and was given mega vitamins to correct it. I took everything in the hopes of regaining my health – nothing worked. All the vitamins left my belly distended and made me feel bloated. More importantly, my physical state did not improve. It was very disheartening but we kept searching.

I tried many different herbs to help resolve my patchy sleep without success. I was grateful for the few hours I got each night but knew the weakness in my immune system was in part due to my insomnia.

I vowed to never touch another medication and persevered through the physical weakness. I had hopes that I would find the answer as long as I didn't lose my trust. The journey taught me that unexpected gifts were waiting as long as I continued the quest.

•   •   •

I still had the comps to take for the final component of my Masters Degree in Film Studies. I wasn't sure if I would ever work in the industry as I had a career path in mind, but I was determined to finish my degree, even if I never used it.

I pulled out all my coursework and books to prepare for the grueling exam. I planted myself in the office, ready to devote a week or two to the process, and wrap up my graduate work, as I was eager to get back to the lectures. I opened each book and review material and sat there dumbfounded.

The words on the page looked foreign, as if I had never studied the material. Convinced I somehow missed an important course, I retrieved a copy of my transcript and was confused. Not only had I taken the course, but I had received an A. Baffled, I began to hunt through additional materials still thinking that maybe I just needed a refresher.

With each passing curriculum the reality began to settle. I felt a cold chill race through my body as the realization permeated my resistance. My entire graduate degree was completed under the influence of drugs. I knew that illegal drugs could interfere with cognitive function, but it never occurred to me that legal medications could have the same effect. But my mind didn't care that they were prescription drugs – it confused the way in which I stored the information. No matter how I tried, I could not access the knowledge.

I began to research the brain and the process used to store and recall data. Each layer of investigation drove the point home. I could not complete my Masters.

The next realization made me weep. We have millions of children worldwide who are told that drugs will treat their hyperactivity or inability to concentrate. They are told the drugs will improve their grades. How criminal.

Chapter 133

After the disappointment over my graduate work, I focused my energy on developing my new vision – to speak out on the dangers of prescription and illegal drugs.

I saw the way advertising distorted the truth of the common ailments and offered only medications to treat the unsuspecting public. I doubted the doctors were aware that they were prescribing drugs that could keep their patients hooked for life? I suspected very few physicians knew, as most were in the business of healing rather than harming. They were offering what they thought was the best treatment today.

However, I did have the fervent belief that many in the field of psychiatry had become too closely tied to the use of mind-altering drugs. My experience with Dr. Braun was crashing wilding in my brain as the magnitude of the statistics flowed across my computer screen.

I was curious when the trend toward mass drugging occurred, and read hundreds of articles on how the FDA re-leased the standards on Direct-to-Consumer marketing in 1997. Only a few countries allowed the drug companies to peddle their products on television, for a very good reason. It was too easy for the consumer to buy into the pretty ads and think that they could have the cure that was portrayed on television. It was always pills.

Even doctors complained that their patients would ask for drugs by name, thinking they fit the symptoms on television. I started watching the drug ads carefully and saw how they alluded to definitive science, yet always treated the symptoms only. I remember all too well how my insomnia, anxiety and depression were treated – with psychoactive drugs. When was it acceptable to treat only symptoms, rather than locating the actual cause?

As the layers of research unfolded, the magnitude of the issue became incomprehensible. The statistics rolled out that included 8.5 million children on stimulant class drugs to treat hyperactivity. I wondered if the parents knew the medication they fed their children was similar to crystal meth.

Nearly half the American public was on an antidepressant and untold numbers of our elderly were taking tranquilizers. I questioned how many were misdiagnosed with Alzheimer's, but were actually having a side effect or were in withdrawal. I recalled my memory loss and inability to concentrate. I couldn't help but recall the horrible withdrawals and wonder how many would survive.

I saw that during the last century, illegal drugs were used to treat symptoms of depression, anxiety and symptoms of hyperactivity. Even infants and children were given cocaine and heroin to treat toothaches or nervousness.

I saw how the manufacturers of Bayer Aspirin sold heroin in the last century. I saw ad campaigns from the 1900's where Sigmund Freud as well as Pope Leo touted the value of cocaine. Would our recent drug ads be archived to reveal how our society had declined?

The information was fascinating but also terrifying. I wondered how the war on drugs could miss such an obvious target?

Then I began to research what could be causing all the symptoms of depression, anxiety, hyperactivity and insomnia. The results had me smashing my fist on the desk.

Slowly I gained an understanding of how various vitamin deficiencies looked the same as mental illness. I began to grasp the importance of not treating only a symptom, but rather locating the cause of illness.

I have to admit that I didn't understand this for years and bought into the magic pill theory. Instead, they became the silver bullets that nearly took my life.

I used to feel that if the symptom was removed then it was a cure. I couldn't have been more misguided. I finally understood that whatever was out of balance would continue to decline and unfortunately, the effects of the pill would complicate the recovery.

What I also didn't grasp for years was the fact that our bodies are wonderful and highly skilled machines. We each have the basic requirements for survival that include air, water, vitamins and minerals. But we also have a unique symphony of chemicals that comprise the individual balance. Some need more protein, others specific vitamins. When did it become acceptable treatment to assume that the whole of society was Serotonin deficient, particularly when too many ailments caused depression?

Each layer of information brought waves of anger. Symptoms of wheat intolerance included chronic fatigue, irritability, schizophrenia, weakness and headaches. Iron and zinc deficiencies caused fatigue, weight loss, irritability, mental confusion, poor cognitive function, and emotional disturbances - many of the symptoms of ADHD.

Even an Omega 3 deficiency could cause the most serious condition such as post-partum depression. How many women even knew this information, and instead turned to drugs thinking they were protecting their babies.

The realization that a vitamin B deficiency could be the root of my problems made me feel faint. The list read like my history – depression, anxiety, paranoia, fatigue, degeneration of spine and suicidal thoughts. My god – why didn't the medical community know this? But the question remained on why I was not utilizing all the B vitamins I had taken over the years. I should be rich in B vitamins as I took them every day. I was convinced there was still a critical piece of the puzzle missing.

Chapter 134

As my awareness deepened, so did my anger toward Dr. Braun for looking only to drugs as the answer. Quickly I realized that he was not the exception, but rather the rule. Very few doctors even understood the importance of nutrition or had schooling in that area.

Yet many physical illnesses such as Candida, Thyroid malfunctions or Diabetes also looked like mental illness. The influx of HMO's into America made it difficult for physicians to take the time to properly assess their patients. I had a girl-friend who was a doctor and lost her job because she spent too much time with her patients. How could a doctor, who is taught to scientifically evaluate their patients, complete a physical and diagnose in a few minutes time. All most had time for was a prescription. They had been duped into fast medicine as well.

I began to see that it was the same game as the last century, just improved marketing that drove sales today. I remembered seeing the early antidepressant ads while in the midst of the legal proceedings. The image of a beautiful woman enjoying life with a handsome and kind man had powerful appeal.

Or the bouncing cartoon character with a cloud over his head that magically vanished after taking an antidepressant. It was embarrassing that I ever bought into the hype.

When the FDA allowed direct-to-consumer marketing for prescription drugs, it became a powerful marketing tool. Sales soared and millions of people reached for the lovely little pills. Like myself, many became trapped by the illusion of happiness and headed into the grips of addiction.

I wondered how many made it out.

Just as quickly as my anger rose toward the medical community, it subsided. I could not blame it solely on them. Each of us is ultimately responsible for our decisions and I was more than willing to look for a quick fix. Many people just like myself will reach for anything when day after day the depression deepens. I also know that drug advertising gives the perception that prescriptions are the answer to what ails us. It is so easy to reach for the pretty little pills rather than continue to search for the underlying cause. Until we get into trouble.

As consumers, we drive every product in a free market society and eventually must look to ourselves for the decline of our own culture. If we did not buy into the quick fix theory, the drug companies would not continue to flood the market with multitudes of prescriptions that only mask a symptom rather than treat the root cause.

I did not want to continue to hunt for the root of my problems. I bought into the idea that a tiny pill could fix me. If one pill couldn't, why in the world did I ever believe that thousands could?

I hold each of us culpable in this scam. The drug companies rank supreme for hiding the truth about the side effects and addictive nature to many of the psychiatric drugs. It was not until recent years that they even admitted many psychiatric medications could cause suicidal ideation. And to think these meds are given for depression. Was I the only one who saw the flagrant contradictions?

I blame the politicians for not protecting the unsuspecting public. I condemn the FDA, as they are the governing body that should be aware of the blatant misrepresentations and hold the drug companies liable.

I am angry at hospitals and the physicians for buying into quick medicine that does not promote preventative medicine and only treats the disease model.

Psychiatry should be ashamed at their willingness to label common ailments as mental illness, and as a result prescribe medications that could alter the course of our lives. When did a symptom alone become a disease? When did the medical profession allow an illness that could not be verified? The chemical imbalance theory is just that – pure conjecture on what is causing depression and anxiety.

The insurance companies are also in the thick of the con as many will not cover a Naturopath or an individual schooled in nutrition. When did prevention take a back seat to illness?

And ultimately, I blame the public for believing in clever marketing campaigns and speedy health. There is no substitute for good health and we should demand more from the manufacturers. Whether it is food, medicine or vitamins, we have the right as the consumer to demand quality and proof of their claims. When is the last time any of us reviewed the list of side effects or interactions in a bottle of ibuprofen? Like myself, most take the nuisance sheet out and throw it away. We just assume it's safe. Why?

When did we accept lower quality foods, stripped of nutritional value? We feed our children sugar and white flour products and then wonder why they display symptoms of hyperactivity or depression. We will not fix what ails our society until we each stiffen our level of responsibility and refuse to take less than what is ideal for our families.

The consumer has the ultimate power and we have all forgotten that rule in commerce. Without our money, trade would freeze. Why did we forget that we have tremendous control over the economy? It is time for us to demand change from others and ourselves.

We must protect the next generation for they are our future, and they are at risk.

Chapter 135

I worked on booking lectures to a few colleges in Los Angeles and the students responded. After the first dozen lectures I began to incorporate more of my personal story, including many of my embarrassing moments on the drugs. I was brutally honest about my memory and contemptuous attitude. I poured out my health issues and took them through my decline. Then I walked them through the withdrawal process and the terror I experienced. They begged for help as most were on the drugs and like myself, could not quit without suffering. I encouraged them to see a naturopath to determine what vitamins and minerals were missing in their diet.

The new lecture presentation held the audience riveted. There were no more glazed looks and instead, they sat on the edge of their seats to not miss a word. It was working.

The difficult part was booking the lectures. Many professors or businesses did not think prescription pills were a problem, only illegal drugs and alcohol. It was frustrating and left me concerned that only a smattering of audiences would ever hear my experience.

I could not have predicted what was coming.

MJ heard of a sauna program that could eliminate the toxins from the body. It utilized niacin; oils and vitamins to ensure the body could release the toxins while the heat of the sauna opened the pores. We both knew I was pickled as years of surgery, working in the chemical industry and the prescription drugs had left my skin yellow. My liver functions were within normal range, but I knew better.

Although the addiction to the drugs had been conquered at Cirque Lodge, I could still feel the effects on my nervous system. My memory was poor and my physical state very weak. I prayed the sauna could restore me to a state of health.

I started the five-hour a day commitment, thinking any advancement of the lectures would have to wait until I finished the program. Each day was a struggle as toxins began to pour out of my body.

I began with 100 mg. of niacin and my body flushed head to toe as it reacted with the toxins. I saw old sunburns from bathing suits I had not worn in decades, surface and fade away as the program continued.

I saw a woman sweat green paint, and was told it was the primary color that she and her husband manufactured. Her white towel turned colors for days and then finally stopped. I smelled heavy concentrations of chlorine emanate from a man who was a swimmer and had spent hours in the pool each morning.

I saw my fresh white towels turn shades of brown and grey as the poisons melted out of my body. I felt years of chemicals and anesthesia, drugs and other poisons exit my being. I relived ecstasy and felt the pain of the spinal injections heighten and then leave. I felt the effects of the antidepressants, tranquilizers and pain killers come to the surface and dissolve before I finished for the day. Each day I inched my way toward a clean body.

I met some lovely people, all seeking freedom from their toxins. I laughed and cried as the experiences that were tied to the toxin were released. It was an odd sensation to have the emotion surface and clear within hours. There were no repetitive thoughts or fear, just a release.

I truly enjoyed the company of the staff and guests, but it was a connection I made in the third week that would change my life forever.

Chapter 136

*T*here were days where conversation became quite intense, as we spent over five hours a day together, and had time to thrash out ideas. One night a discussion ensued on truly evil people. The root of the disagreement was whether sociopaths could blend into normal society or whether their psychosis would be apparent. Many felt that their insanity must be visible and therefore, it was unreasonable that a psychopath could hide within a culture.

I became frustrated with their naivety and proceeded to tell the group about my experience with Mark. I don't know why, as this was the first time I had shared part of my story since leaving Cirque. But before I reached the end of the story, my time in the sauna was over for the day. I packed up and left the group with stunned expressions, as I existed the hot box.

The next day a petite, beautiful, blond woman approached me and stated that she heard about my story. She asked to hear it in its entirety.

Andrea owned a fashion house and had been extremely successful in the world of fashion for many years. Although she hadn't taken any prescription drugs, she had experimented with Ecstasy in her teens. In her early twenties, she suffered panic attacks due to her hectic schedule and poor eating habits and was prescribed Xanax. She chose not to take them and instead changed her lifestyle to include exercise and organic food and the symptoms melted away.

The sauna program made sense to her and she decided to take a few weeks away from her crazy schedule in San Francisco to come to Los Angeles and do the program.

For some unknown reason, I trusted this woman and felt the need to tell her my whole story. We spent the entire 5 hours talking and I shared all the details of my past, including the conviction and restitution order.

I disclosed elements of my research and imparted my experience in withdrawals and how I was lecturing to local colleges. She was riveted and listened to each piece of information without interrupting. When I was finished, she peppered me with questions and I could see her brilliant mind clipping away. It was as if the floodgates opened for her and she couldn't absorb the information quickly enough.

It was truly a remarkable conversation that left me energized when normally I was exhausted from hours in the sauna. This was one of those unique exchanges that left me knowing my life was about to detonate.

By the end of the day a rare bond had formed that will last a lifetime. It was as if we had been friends for decades as the comfort between us was astonishing. I was struck with the deep sensation that we were brought together for a very specific purpose.

Not only was she non judgmental about my history, she embraced it. She was struck by the magnitude of the drug problem and the way in which society reached for pills or other drugs. It also touched a deep cord in her, as she had a couple relatives that were prescribed anti-psychotic and antidepressant medications and had terrible results. She watched as their lives melted away and the shell that remained was through a drug-induced haze. It angered her that millions of people were being subjected to a cocktail of drugs in an experiment that many would not survive.

Andrea is one of the rare beings that grace this planet. She is absolutely beautiful and looks as if she should be on the silver screen – and of course she doesn't see it. But that is by far the smaller piece of the puzzle as she is kind, dedicated and absolutely brilliant in business. Her sense of humor is unfailing and her loyalty extreme. She has a deep well of caring for humanity and found that personal success could not be gratifying while so many were suffering.

I never had to ask Andrea to join me. It was as natural as breathing. We just stepped into a rhythm and got to work. I found not only my business partner, but also a very dear friend who I will cherish forever.

One week later, Andrea left a seventeen-year career in the world of fashion, and together we founded *Label Me Sane*, an organization committed to changing public perception regarding all drugs.

Andrea finished the sauna program before I did, and went back to San Francisco to finalize her business before moving to Los Angeles. I remained and felt the years of accumulated toxins drain out of my body. It left me feeling light and clear-headed and my ability to write returned.

Chapter 137

Andrea and I spent hours on the phone strategizing how to proceed. She collected my months of research and took the volumes of data back to San Francisco. She was a sponge for information and took my research and delved deeper. She drove back to Los Angeles to meet me several times before she moved down. We spent hours working on our line of attack.

She had stacks of pads with a litany of questions, facts, and ideas. Her research was impeccable and she could not absorb the information quickly enough.

Within a few weeks she moved to Los Angeles and we both moved to Malibu. We wanted the beach to envelope us through business and our homes.

Then we set a course into action to expand the lecture, and deliver it to as many venues as possible.

The lecture was developed into the exquisite work we use today. It covers all aspects of illegal and legal drugs, the marketing campaigns used to sell drugs and addresses nutritional deficiencies that mimic symptoms of depression, anxiety and Attention Deficit Hyperactivity Disorder (ADHD). It incorporates the history of illegal drugs and the development of today's campaign.

Then we tackled how to expand the audience base, including adult populations within all walks of life. It was our fervent belief that if parents were brought into awareness, they would never drug their children. We were determined to free as many people as possible off the drugs, thus releasing their voices to inspire others.

During the development, we were searching my medical records for the diagnoses that were given to me during the time I was suffering from mercury poisoning. The discovery appalled both of us as my labels included Clinical Depression, Anxiety Disorder, Post Traumatic Stress Disorder, Obsessive Compulsive and about twenty others that allowed the drugging to continue.

I never understood labeling, but the reality sent a chill up my spine. In order to be prescribed medications, one must first receive a label. Whether for an infection, bronchitis, cancer, diabetes, or HIV, the *label* is given and then the medication is prescribed.

However, what was happening with mental illness symptoms was entirely different. These represent our mental state and therefore our perceived effectiveness in society. Once we are given a label that represents mental illness, many doctors refuse to look further to discover the root of the problem. We are judged based on those labels and can lose valuable opportunities. This is a vicious cycle that leaves many drugged for life and carrying labels that imply they are unstable. Then of course the drugs increase the instability and the cocktail of drugs are increased.

Children that are labeled and drugged may be restricted from entering the field of law enforcement or the military and a plethora of other careers because their mental state is deemed unsound.

I had a woman in an early lecture state she was in the nursing program and given an antidepressant. When she completed her education, she could not be licensed in her state due to her mental illness label.

Another man stated that his dream was to be a police officer, but could not pass his background investigation due to the antidepressant he was prescribed.

I couldn't help but wonder if parents knew they were preventing life choices for their children by allowing the use of many of these medications.

I was misdiagnosed due to mercury poisoning, but the mental illness labels were given in abundance. They imply a woman of instability rather than someone who was given a toxic substance. Even after my auto accident, I suffered terrible depression and anxiety. I have not found those records but I suspect they are riddled with reports of my mental decline. When did it become abnormal to feel loss?

When my father died, I had months of deep grief. I loved my father and felt his loss to my core. I did not realize that I received a label of Grief Disorder until much later.

In time, my sadness lifted and I was able to think of him with fondness, without the deep well of tears I suffered in the first few weeks after his death. Why would such a huge loss be considered a mental illness? It angered me, as it is implied that somehow my reaction was anything but human. It was the response of a loving daughter who missed her father. When did that become abnormal?

I am a firm believer that we must be evaluated on our merit rather than a perception of conduct. I have learned all too well the danger of diagnosing through behavior alone.

Chapter 138

*T*he next four months brought a hectic pace as we were lecturing more frequently, while establishing our new company through an Internet presence.

It did not seem to matter where we lectured, whether at colleges or universities, businesses, attorneys, professional groups or parents – the results were the same. The rooms were filled with people from all walks of life, every ethnicity and economic group, and they all had stories. Our surveys indicated that anywhere between 70-90% of the rooms were either on the drugs, or had an immediate family member who was.

Although a small number were on illegal drugs, the majority was taking various prescription medications and begged us for help. Like me, they had started on the drugs unaware of how addictive they were. No one realized they received a mental illness label prior to being prescribed. Most had received their prescriptions from their doctor rather than a psychiatrist, and somehow thought it would insulate them from a label that suggested mental illness. Just like myself, they had no idea any of the information in our lecture existed, even though the web was full of documentation. They all felt deceived. They rushed us for help to withdraw and return to a state of health. At this point we did not have a solution, other then to quit cold-turkey in treatment. I knew few could afford it even if they could survive.

I was interviewed on numerous radio shows in both the United States and England. Our exposure grew tenfold but the nagging question remained on how to withdraw safely. It left us troubled.

I knew how dangerous these drugs were and our lecture conveyed the point thoroughly. What I didn't expect was the massive response of people who had attempted to stop the drugs and couldn't. I didn't know what to tell them, as most couldn't afford treatment or the ability to separate from the world as I had. They were mothers, attorneys and professionals who desperately wanted an answer.

However, it was after a presentation at a school of Naturopathy that we actually stopped lecturing for a few months. The lecture started like any other - around 100 students and two professors were present. Generally, for anyone in the natural healing arts, the purpose of our lecture was to inform them of what their future clients may describe.

Both Andrea and myself fully expected this to be a biased audience, as they would already understand the importance of not just drugging symptoms. We anticipated a bit of disinterest or boredom.

But as I spoke, the room became exceedingly quiet. A couple of girls started to cry in earnest and others leaned forward on their chairs. The two professors moved in closer.

As I closed the lecture, the students raced up to talk to both of us. They begged for help to withdraw off antidepressants and benzos. They pleaded for solutions. One girl took me outside and sobbed as she thought I was telling her story. My personal experience had moved them into action, but we had no solutions to offer.

Here we were, among students of naturopathy and nearly every person in the room, including the two professors, was on some type of behavioral drug – and they were all asking for help. We felt as if we let them down.

Andrea and I drove from the lecture and sat at the beach. We were despondent and vowed that we would not address another group until we had a viable solution. I understood perfectly the withdrawals and had tried a multitude of nutritional products when I tried to taper, without success. Most were expensive and only aggravated my withdrawals.

This started a quest of available programs. We were disappointed time and again. Many I had tried while in withdrawal without success. Some individuals we spoke to had no thorough understanding of prescription drugs or the extended withdrawal syndrome. They were only selling products to a desperate public. We continued to search.

When I left the sauna program, my heart felt lighter than it had in many years. I was convinced the drug toxins were gone but I still felt depleted. I spent hundreds of dollars on vitamins and took piles of them daily. Before bedtime I took a collection of vitamins and herbs in an attempt to sleep more than a few hours. Andrea would laugh at me and strongly questioned all the stacks of vitamins. Yet she saw that night after night I wouldn't sleep and was always exhausted.

Many days I would work only a few hours, then have to leave to ice my back, as the pain made it intolerable to sit up for extended periods. She knew my underlying issue had yet to be resolved and if we could find a way to address my health, we would have an answer for others.

I tried every product that had potential to see if it could help me. Nothing did. I was still struggling with reoccurring colds and my immune system was exceptionally weak. I was piling in vitamins and minerals in an attempt to nourish my body – all to no avail.

Then we found it.

Chapter 139

After months of exhausting research and failed attempts, Andrea and I met a man who had been researching how psychiatric drugs were metabolized and the way to overcome the withdrawal symptoms. There were many interesting tidbits of information, but it was the mention of Glutathione that peaked our interest. Neither of us had heard of the master antioxidant and wanted more information.

Although he sounded knowledgeable, we went back and performed our own research to verify his claims. The data available was fascinating and in abundance. Since the early 1980's a team of scientists have been evaluating the necessity of Glutathione in the body and the effects of depletion. They have also worked on specific ways to raise Glutathione levels in a way the body could readily recognize.

The early research indicated clinical studies on patients suffering from HIV and Cancer. By increasing intracellular Glutathione, patients were surviving longer as their immune system was strengthened.

Glutathione is in every cell, but has particularly high concentrations in the liver, as it is the organ that is involved in detoxification and elimination of toxic materials, such as drugs. These were the studies that sharpened our interest. As the level of pollution increased worldwide, the demand within the body for adequate levels of Glutathione amplified.

However, it could not be taken in an external form as the body needed to manufacture Glutathione on the cellular level to ensure the cells could build up an adequate store. The molecule size of Glutathione in a pill form was too large for the body to convert.

What came from all the research was awareness that the ability to taper an individual off psychiatric medication was possible as long as sufficient levels of Glutathione were present. This would mean the side effects would diminish while the withdrawal process was occurring.

We were hopeful but still kept a fair amount of skepticism. We did not want to endorse a taper program that could not deliver, as like myself, most people were desperate.

One afternoon I had a terrible cold and we had a long meeting. I tired quickly and mentioned that I had been having trouble sleeping. A man left the room and returned with a plastic container half filled with a specific cherry extract. He told me to take a tablespoon in water before bedtime.

I tried the cherry extract but did not feel any results. I was deflated and gave up after two days. The next time I saw him I mentioned the poor results. He laughed and said that it wasn't like benzos. I had to stay on it for a while to see results.

Sure enough, after ten days I slept through the night. Encouraged, I called him and asked what else he recommended. He recommended a powdered product that would raise intracellular Glutathione. I mixed it in water a couple times a day and was determined to see it through.

My body responded instantly and the results were so

phenomenal that within one week both Andrea and MJ commented on the difference. My energy soared and in the two years, I have only had one cold that did not develop into bronchitis or pneumonia. That was a clear indicator that my body was healing.

It was as if my body was craving the right nutrients and was so grateful when I finally nourished it properly. My back began to heal and the pain started to diminish. The swelling in my joints melted away and the stiffness that had plagued me for decades shifted back to normal movement.

I began to crave the taste of the products and rarely missed a dose. My sleep became deep and consistent and I knew unequivocally, that even after 34 surgeries, I could heal.

I had been in physical therapy since leaving Cirque Lodge, but was having a very difficult time making progress. After implementing a few simple suggestions, my program improved. Mobility began to soar and with it, a true sense that I could recover.

Chapter 140

Then we heard of various types of DNA testing that both tested the metabolic pathways in the liver that many psychiatric drugs traveled, and also various genetic markers to determine what variations could predict future disease and assist in determining exactly what nutritional requirements each person had based on their individual DNA.

We were told how a large percentage of the public had genetic variations in the most basic areas, such as vitamin B deficiency. This particular genetic variation makes it impossible for them to metabolize B vitamins in a pill form. The body viewed the vitamin as a toxin and just passed it. Research was done for ways that an individual could metabolize the critical B vitamins but in a source the body would not view as a toxin.

Andrea and I began researching this information on DNA testing and the way variations were affecting the public. We suspected that many individuals who were prescribed psychiatric pills may have this variation as one of the symptoms of vitamin B deficiency is depression.

It was recommended Andrea and I take a DNA Nutritional Test to determine exactly what my body could and could not metabolize. We did it without hesitation.

The results were startling. I finally understood not only

what was wrong with my body, but also why I could never heal with even with all the vitamins I took on a regular basis.

My testing revealed that I had a genetic variation that made it impossible for me to metabolize both B vitamins and Calcium. No matter how many vitamins I took, my body could not metabolize them. All the piles of vitamins were useless for me. The only way my body could correct the deficiency was with superfoods, rich in B vitamins that my body could then metabolize, as it would bypass the genetic variation.

I added various items to my regimen and within four months I felt like a new woman. My body became strong and any remnants of cloudiness in my mind cleared completely. My nails stopped peeling and the dark circles under my eyes faded. My memory improved dramatically as well as my stamina. And finally I could sit up for extended periods without the excruciating pain in my back. As my energy increased, so did my interest and belief in a possible withdrawal program.

The yellow tones to my skin returned to pink and the deep wrinkles in my face and neck diminished. All the strange blemishes that had plagued me through the withdrawals were gone and my hair returned to its rich and thick texture of decades ago.

Andrea's Nutritional test showed the identical B variation that I had, but it also indicated a detox variation. It was especially important for her to keep her Glutathione levels high to support her liver. She started on the products shortly after me and felt her already healthy body, increase in energy. We were working seven days a week and maintaining the pace without effort.

It became so clear to us that what we are passing from generation to generation is not mental illness, but rather genetic variations and deficiencies that are being misdiagnosed. It was time to expose the truth.

Chapter 141

The FDA had listed a tapering regimen for Paxil that stated a reduction schedule over a number of weeks. We used the research performed by others for both the taper program as well as the products that would raise Glutathione levels and provide the necessary nutrients.

We cannot take credit for the taper in any way. What Andrea and I did was to compile the information in an easy to read format and make the taper and products available to the public throughout the world. We did not write the taper, another researcher did. But it was our efforts that brought the taper to the public, in the means of an easy to use workbook.

I had always dreamed of an organization that could inspire and provide support for those caught in the clutch of addiction. What Andrea and I envisioned together was the way *Label Me Sane* could be expanded worldwide. We wanted the message to reach those that didn't realize the drugs were contributing to their feelings of depression and anxiety. We also wanted to provide an organization that could offer hope from others that had traversed the road before them. Finally, we wanted people to combine their voice with ours and help change this horrific drugging trend.

We decided to start one of our clients on the taper program as we was now convinced the products were legitimate.

She was a woman in the Midwest named Kristin, who had been on Prozac and Klonopin for five years. She had tried multiple times to get off the drugs but each time she tried, her world went black. She had a little girl that she couldn't feel love toward and literally was losing her hope of ever being free.

We started her on the program and within three weeks she emailed a thank you, stating that she finally saw the flowers in her yard and had played with her daughter for the first time in years. In a short period of time she was off the drugs completely and back in full swing of her life.

I was finally a believer.

·   ·   ·

We started other clients on the program and the results were the same as Kristin. They all began to feel their health improve and were withdrawing safely, without the horrific symptoms I had experienced.

When we initially endorsed the workbook, it was important to combine clinical information for any physician to scientifically understand the basis of the taper. But it was even more important to provide a lifeline to those on the drugs. Therefore, I wrote the introduction to offer hope to those still suffering and Andrea wrote the closing chapter asking for individuals to speak out once they completed the program.

Within ten weeks of its release, people were tapering off prescriptions drugs in every state in the United States and on three continents.

Our phones exploded overnight and we couldn't get product quickly enough to help everyone. Our lectures, radio and television interviews reached the masses worldwide.

Chapter 142

Both Andrea and I developed some remarkable friend-ships with a few of our clients. We shared their darkest hours and also their ascent toward life. As a result, the bonds we formed have been life changing for all of us. We are told time and again that it was divine intervention that brought them to us.

Barbara called me three days short of a cold-turkey withdrawal from Klonopin. Her doctor did not understand the withdrawals and not only had her on three psychiatric medica-tions, but was cutting her doses too rapidly. She was so fright-ened and the conversation was mainly to provide support. We sent her package overnight and she began the program instant-ly.

I helped her locate a doctor that would work closely with her through the taper, while I provided the nutritional support. Some days she called several times and I even broke a cardinal rule about giving out my cell phone number. I have done it a few times and have never regretted it. There are in-stances when a call on the weekend is enough to keep someone connected to life. She is nearly finished with the program and we have a friendship that transcends the distance between us. But now she feels wonderful and we share the lightness of life, rather than the pain.

Andrea had a call that made tears stream down her face. Walter was suicidal and felt he could not live any longer. He was on a cocktail of antidepressants and benzos, and had lost his job due to his declining mental state. Andrea spent hours on the phone with him, gently guiding him toward the program. He was skeptical and a bit aggressive, yet believed she might be able to help him. *Label Me Sane* was his last hope. Within weeks he was feeling so wonderful that he gave the products to his son who had been placed in a facility, due to his outbursts in school. His son responded as quickly as Walter had, and not only was he discharged home, but re-entered the public school system. Within a month, Walter landed a wonderful job and was able to save his home. His gratitude was overwhelming and during the last conversation Andrea once again cried, but this time they were tears of joy.

Sherry called full of aggression and suspicion, but also pleading for help. She was prescribed the drugs for the symptoms of menopause. She had a host of side effects and felt her life slipping away. She no longer felt the connection to her charming husband and daughter, and was terrified. She also felt deeply betrayed by the medical profession.

I spent an inordinate amount of time helping her through her program. We took out foods and herbs that were causing an adverse reaction, and one day it just clicked into gear. She called a while back and I steeled myself for another round of aggression. Instead, what I received was not only a thank you from both Sherry and her family, but also an offer to help expand the *Label Me Sane* message. Sherry had her life back and like me, she wanted to help another. Now she is a passionate, wonderful woman, completely committed to the fight. That is the cycle of what we do here. We offer hope and bring the thread back between each of us.

There is gratitude, hope and true appreciation for the work we do. There is no way I could ever imagine doing anything else.

And then there are the calls that drive the seriousness of the work home. Last week a man telephoned whose brother committed suicide. He was a seventeen year decorated fireman and had trouble sleeping. He had never taken a drug in his life, and finally accepted a sample his doctor offered for a new sleeping pill. Within a few days, he shot and killed himself in front of his children.

His brother didn't even know why he reached for Andrea, but he just had to talk. Like so many others, he did not know any of these drugs were dangerous. He was numb from grief.

Andrea and I couldn't speak for a long time after his call. We both knew there was so much more we had to do.

Chapter 143

After the initial onslaught of tapers, many individuals wanted to lecture in their community. The grassroots campaign of *Label Me Sane* that we had envisioned, sprung up overnight in communities around the nation.

People were getting healthy on the products just as I had, and were reaching to inspire others. It was working. We were inundated with requests from mothers who wanted to incorporate the products into their family's diet. We began to see people from all walks of life regain their lives and not only taper off their prescriptions safely, but also feel great while doing it.

Doctors and healthcare practitioners began calling for information on how to help their patients. It became so obvious that many did not have any awareness of the addictive nature to these drugs and truly wanted to help. They didn't sign up for fast medicine that hurt rather than helped.

• • •

And yet, through all the amazing success of *Label Me*

Sane, what continues to warm my heart and inspire me are the people calling for help. They reach from all over the globe with the hope of finding their way back to health and life.

I try to take as many calls as possible, as many want to speak to someone who has been through the nightmare – and survived. They draw on my strength just as I drew on the staff of Cirque Lodge. They need the belief from another living soul that they too can make it.

·   ·   ·

And through all the insane work hours, I rescued two abandoned dogs off the edge of the freeway. MJ and I were on our way to dinner, and saw four fearful eyes trying to assess when to cross. We immediately stopped and hustled into a muddy gully to try and find them. It took hours to wrestle them into our car, as they were both terrified. They had been horribly abused but wanted to believe they were safe. MJ already had a cat, so of course, I brought them both home. I immediately called Andrea and asked if she would come over and bring shampoo and dog food. She laughed and appeared within thirty minutes.

The older dog is a Border Collie I named Sky. He was severely wounded and needed gentle nurturing back to health. Like myself, he has had multiple injuries that never healed properly. He has a slight limp and the sweetest face. He stepped into my life and as Selsie had, became my shadow.

The puppy, Tobie, is a firecracker Australian Shepherd, who refuses to see evil in the world. He fell in love instantly with Andrea, who immediately adopted him. His innocence, inquisitive nature and willful spirit make me laugh daily.

They come to the office with us and harass the staff.

Shoes are fiercely protected; as everyone knows they are toast if you kick them off. Tobie has toy boxes and still works to snag an unoccupied shoe. We have to explain to our clients why they hear barking in the background. But Andrea and I work massive hours and do not want to leave the dogs unattended. Like many of us, they did not receive the kindness they should have.

These two wounded souls helped to bring stability to my life. And just like me, they both receive the products in their daily regimen. Every morning, without fail, my living alarm clock wakes me just before 5:00. Sky and I head to the beach to meet Andrea and Tobie. The boys greet each other and race wildly up and down the waters edge with true joy and freedom. Andrea and I plan our day and allow the ocean air to clear our mind and soul, while the dogs fill their fur with sand. Their innocence, trust and tender nature bring laughter each morning. Every day takes them further from their past pain, just as it does me. We all healed together and share an environment of love, trust and kindness.

My connection to the gentle world of nature and animals was finally complete.

Chapter 144

$\mathcal{A}$ distant voice filtered in. I felt a lick across my face as Sky settled next to me. I saw Tobie attacking a bush.

"Alesandra, I thought I'd find you here." Andrea's hand touched my shoulder gently.

I sat up and realized how long I'd been gone.

"Sorry. I lost track of time." I was a little sheepish.

"Hard interview, huh?" She had a gentle look of concern.

"Well, we knew it was coming. It just brought back so many memories." I sat up and locked my arms across my knees.

"You OK?"

"It just took me back through so many years of pain."

I looked up at this special woman - so grateful she entered my life.

"Do you need to talk about it?" Andrea sat down next to me and sat quietly.

"It's strange how much time has passed, and yet every once in a while I get overwhelmed by my history." I leaned my head on my knee.

"You've done an amazing thing, going public with your story." She had such warmth on her face.

"I'm so proud of what we are doing. But…do you think they will accept me when they know the truth?" I had tears in my eyes.

"Absolutely. I did." Andrea had a fierce quality to her words.

"You're rare." I was feeling vulnerable.

"No, I'm not. I just saw the truth and the public will too." She spoke with conviction.

"I hope so." I sat upright and reached to stretch.

"The public wants a champion and you're it. This movement needs a face and you survived for a reason. I wouldn't be here if it wasn't for what you went through. You changed my life!" Her eyes locked mine and I knew she spoke the truth.

"Well, I couldn't have done this without you. Clearly I'm not trustworthy on my own." I gave a light chuckle.

"Clearly." Andrea was laughing too. "Let's change this planet, shall we?"

Andrea stood and reached to help me up. We both started the descent down the hillside and retraced our steps up the beach. Our hair was flying, and together we laughed like children with the dogs racing ahead.

Chapter 145

Was it all worth it?
No question.
Am I a perfect person now?
Far from it.
Do I know the value of feeling the full range of human existence?
To my core.

I have days where my life has a darker shade of gray that I didn't see coming. I experience betrayal and disappointment and I now feel the grief and anger and then move past it. I am grateful for the people surrounding me, and no longer mourn long for those that prove untrustworthy.

I have a group of amazing people that lessen life's misery and expand the joy. They are gifted, tender and have deep wells of concern for all mankind. They trust me with their deepest joy, fear and honor who I am. We spend our days in unabridged laughter and simultaneous tears for those that still suffer.

A few short years ago I thought no one would find value in my presence. I questioned whether any human would ever trust me again or whether my past would overshadow any personal relationship. Now it seems absurd to have ever engaged that thought.

Many that work at *Label Me Sane* could have had inordinate success, and chose instead to spend their days helping people who, like myself, are looking for a thread back to life. We inspire, cajole and often just give an ear to their fears and ultimately, the gift that was bestowed upon me when I went through the horror, is passed to another. That is the true reward of what we do at *Label Me Sane*. We offer hope and the belief that each person can make the journey back to health and in turn, their passion. Many choose to use their voice as I have. There is nothing more magical then to watch the cycle of life continue and see each in their own way, turn to help another.

Our world has changed significantly and one of the great losses for the American culture is the elimination of the family unit and the sense of neighbors. We have become so separate that we often do not share our lives in the way we were meant to. I firmly believe that having a living connection, whether it is in the same city or across the globe, unites us. What we experience every day within our company, is the true feeling of extended family. I receive photos of their children, animals and the joy they share as they live free of the drugs. I receive stories of desperation transformed into hope. There is no finer gift anyone could possibly give me.

Each day takes me further from the darkness and converts my past terror into true elation, for I know what we do here. I am filled with the true belief that it was all worth living. Every black moment brought me closer to my true mission. I now know the power of a dark heart, but I also have the fervent belief that light always perseveres.

I formally changed my name before I ever started the withdrawal process. It was as if I needed the new identity to survive the horror and triumph. Only recently I discovered the true derivation. While I thought Alesandra was a name that meant strength, the Greek meaning is *Defender of Mankind.* My hope is to live up to my name. My old name feels so foreign that I couldn't even use it in this memoir. Alesandra Rain is who I am now, the past must be put to rest.

As for Mark, I do not know what has happened to him. I suspect he is still conning people, as that is his nature. I tried to stop him and failed. I hope that someday someone can. Any remnant of life with him feels like an eternity ago. He has faded away and no longer haunts me. Someday I will remarry and until the right man arrives, my days will be full of accomplishment, appreciation and friendship.

What I do believe is that I survived only to do my work through *Label Me Sane*. It makes all I went through worth every moment of suffering.

Chapter 146

Was I a victim?
Hardly.
Did I suffer?
Without a doubt.

We are a culmination of choices, beliefs and actions. It isn't only the choices that define who we are but our response to each. It is our ability to accept personal responsibility and become a better person for it. It is truly our attitude that allows one to heal and grow. And of course it is our willingness to be social beings and reach to help another.

All drugs separate us from ourselves and ultimately from each other. Without the connection to another living, breathing person, the thread to life grows thin.

We must reach and find those souls of like mind and common goals. We must learn to disagree and hold firm to our convictions while still honoring the beliefs of others. We must learn to face this world with the full range of emotions. Each sensation and perceived pain is part of who we are and should not be dampened or snuffed from existence. We must find the root of why we suffer and move back toward life.

We must not be afraid to live outside the perceived box of life. I am amazed at how unique we each are and yet many strive to change their basic nature. I am an artist, with all that entails. I feel more deeply than most and I express my gifts in a fashion that was deemed abnormal. It isn't. I am a rare and special woman that just lost my way. I see many others just like myself, facing the same challenge – to be who we are and not feel shame for being rare.

I am a better person for what I have endured. My compassion is endless and my belief in the strength of mankind unfailing. How I lost that understanding will forever puzzle me. But like each of us, all I can do is move forward and never forget the value of this massive lesson. I was given a great gift and my appreciation will forever endure.

Label Me Sane, Inc.

30765 Pacific Coast Hwy # 266
Malibu, CA 90265
866.605.2333 toll free within the US
310.457.1701 for International
www.labelmesane.com
email: info@labelmesane.com